ICQ FYI

Instant Communications Online

Your Q&A Guide to ICQ

By Ted Coombs & Roderico DeLeon

ICQ FYI

Library of Congress Catalog Number: 99-068484

ISBN 1-929685-04-1

5   4   3   2   1

Educational facilities, companies, and organizations interested in multiple copies or licensing of this book should contact the publisher for quantity discount information. Training manuals, CD-ROMs, and portions of this book are also available individually or can be tailored for specific needs.

MUSKA&LIPMAN

2645 Erie Avenue, Suite 41
Cincinnati, Ohio 45208
www.muskalipman.com
publisher@muskalipman.com

This book is composed in Glasgow, Helvetica, and Courier typefaces using QuarkXpress 4.1, Adobe PhotoShop 5.0.2, and Adobe Illustrator 8.0. Created in Cincinnati, Ohio, in the United States of America

Credits

Publisher
Andy Shafran

Managing Editor
Hope Stephan

Development & Copy Editor
Bill McManus

Technical Editor
John Russell

Proofreader
Scott MacLean

Cover Designer
John Windhorst

Production Manager
Cathie Tibbetts

Production Team
DOV Graphics
Michelle Frey
John Windhorst

Indexer
Kevin Broccoli

Printer
R.R. Donnelley and Sons

About the Authors

Ted Coombs is the director of SCIENCE.ORG, a research and development institute. With his son, he is the digital business columnist for *Byte Magazine* and a contributor to *Microsoft Interactive Developer Magazine*. Roderico DeLeon is an Internet developer and consultant. Also a freelance writer, he has written for a broad audience throughout North and Latin America. Both have used ICQ extensively for business and personal communications from the time ICQ was first released.

Acknowledgments

We would like to thank Cristina for the use of her home in Mexico City while we wrote most of this book. Thanks to Andy for believing in ICQ and our book; Jason for being the international test subject; and all our other friends we've used as examples in this book.

Dedication

To our family

Table of Contents

Section 2 Communicating

Section 3 Customizing ICQ

Section 4 All the Goodies

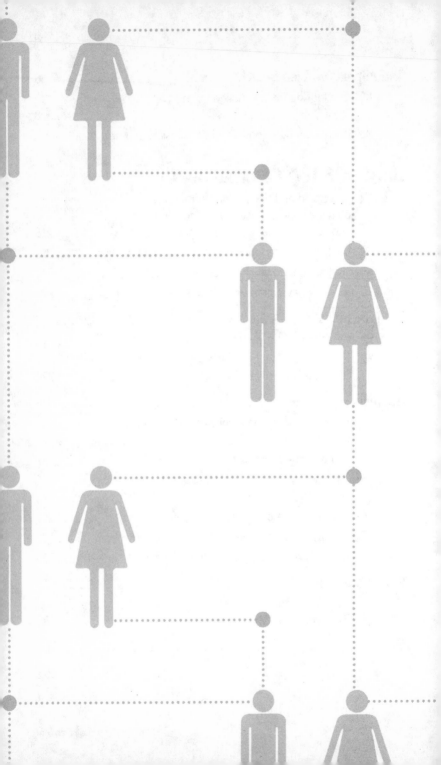

Introduction

ICQ is a wonderful way to communicate with people, either for business or pleasure. It has grown to be one of the most popular ways to chat and send files over the Internet. If you're ready to install ICQ or already have it running, you are one of the many millions who now look to ICQ as their way to communicate with others. This little desktop instant messenger has grown over the years and is now filled with features, utilities, sounds, icons, and integration with the World Wide Web.

The folks who created ICQ, a small group from Israel, have a certain mentality—cram as much into a small space as possible. This mentality has guided the development of both the ICQ program and the ICQ Web page. This book acts as a navigator for beginners and veteran ICQ users through this now jam-packed communications program and to the growing number of Web-based ICQ utilities. Learn all the new ICQ features, and basics for creating and enhancing your ICQ home page. Create your own or join communities with the new ActiveList feature.

ICQ is great for people of all ages, and we offer guides, hints, and suggestions for parents whose children use ICQ. A new world of communities has formed around ICQ. These communities are as diverse as communities in the physical world that has adopted it as their communicator.

We provide all this information in a special question-and-answer format. We think that listing the most common questions that new and experienced ICQ users might ask, and then answering them, is the best way to learn how to use ICQ to the fullest.

Conventions used in this book

Features throughout the book, such as sidebars exploring specific topics in more detail and Tips, Notes, and Cautions, are meant to draw your attention to interesting and often important information. You'll find definitions of key terms in the glossary at the back of the book., and there is also a complete index to help you refer to information readily.

All Web page URLs mentioned in the book appear in **boldface**, as in **www.icq.com**.

Commands are shown in **bold** type. New terms are introduced in *italic* type, and you'll find definitions of all these terms in the Glossary, as well as a complete index, at the end of *ICQ FYI*.

Besides these terminological and typographic conventions, the book also features the following special displays for different types of important text:

TIP

Text formatted like this offers a helpful tip relevant to the topic being discussed in the main text.

NOTE

Text formatted like this highlights other interesting or useful information that relates to the topic under discussion in the main text.

CAUTION

Warnings about actions or operations that could make irreversible changes to your files or might lead to consequences that are potentially harmful are displayed as a "CAUTION." Be sure to read CAUTION text—it can help you to avoid some troublesome pitfalls!

Section 1
Getting ICQ Happy

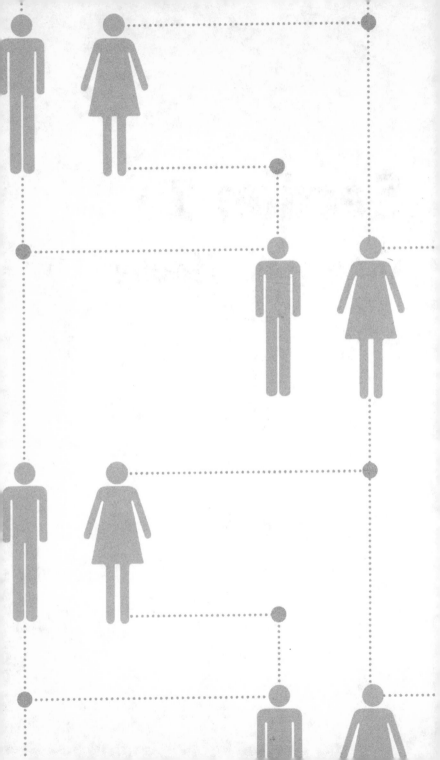

Getting ICQ Happy

An Introduction to ICQ

Smaller and faster is the goal of just about every industry. The Internet is certainly no exception to that trend. Not only has it become the largest storehouse of the world's information, the Internet is rapidly becoming the primary method of worldwide business and personal communications. E-mail revolutionized the way people interact, and now ICQ has taken communications to the next level. Communicating instantly with others over the Internet using this small, fast, messenger application is once again changing the world.

Today, a variety of instant messaging programs is available on the Internet. ICQ is different from these other programs, because even though its humble beginning was as an instant messenger, it has grown into a full-featured business communications tool. In this section, we help you get started with ICQ. You will learn how to download and install the program, get it configured, and add friends and associates to an ICQ Contact List. We also help you to get comfortable with ICQ. Like any communications tool, ICQ involves how people interact with you, and it's important to feel comfortable with the way it is configured so that you don't become overwhelmed with too much communication or feel limited because you aren't able to communicate enough.

The only limit to how much you can communicate with others on the Internet is you. The number of people with whom you can communicate is unlimited. Tens of millions of people around the world use ICQ. You can find someone to chat with in almost any language on almost any topic at any time of the day or night. Entire communities of people have formed around interest groups that send messages and chat using ICQ. Not only can you make new friends, it is no longer uncommon to find romance on the Internet. Many relationships form and blossom using ICQ as an initial way to communicate before meeting. Relationships between individuals in different countries, rarely possible before, are now not only possible but happen every day.

ICQ is an interesting phenomenon. People have had the ability to communicate with others in real time, and anywhere in the world, for many years. The cost of the telephone, however, has always been prohibitive, and the telephone has never had a mechanism to allow for random chats (unless you were a prankster) or for people with a common interest to meet and share. The other problem with the telephone is that no method exists to know ahead of time whether someone is home before calling them. ICQ not only solves that problem of communicating with its built-in tools, it also solves that problem for the telephone. ICQ lets you know whether someone is home and online. Of course, this could mean that the person's phone line is tied up. Yet this is no longer a given. More and more people are accessing the Internet by using their cable systems or installing digital subscriber lines (DSLs) that provide high-speed and dedicated access to the Internet.

ICQ, aside from being your online communicator (**Figure 1.1**), also includes many personal assistant features such as a To Do list, a place to keep notes, a reminder system, an e-mail program, and a phone "follow me" system. Use these features in your home or business to help organize your day, never forgetting your partner's birthday again!

Figure 1.1 The ICQ communicator: so many communication options in such a small package.

No matter how you use the Internet, chances are good that you'll find one of the ICQ features to be so useful that you will use it every day. The more you use ICQ, the more it will become a part of your life. On a rainy day, as you stare through the window next to your computer wondering who else is out there, you will smile when the little "Uh oh" sound of ICQ lets you know that someone knows you're there.

Q1 What does ICQ stand for?

Ham radio operators, searching the air waves for people to communicate with, tapped out the Morse code dot dot, dash dot dash dot, dash dash dot dash, spelling the letters I C Q, which is ham radio operator code for "I Seek You." Endlessly through long nights, ham operators were able to connect with people all over the world, finding new friends in either their own country or other parts of the world. When the night conditions were just right, the upper atmosphere would bounce radio waves a great distance, allowing communication with others far away, sharing their thoughts or just chatting for fun. The Internet isn't perfect, but we no longer have to wait for fickle weather conditions to be just right to communicate with others around the world.

In much the same way that amateur radio operators were able to communicate over low-frequency radio waves, the Internet has made it possible to communicate with anyone on earth connected to the Internet. Some of the first popular ways to communicate over the Internet were e-mail and chatting with the Internet Relay Chat (IRC) software. Sending messages through e-mail, chatting on IRC, and posting messages on Usenet newsgroups opened an entirely new way to communicate. Most people don't realize it, but all of this was going on long before the World Wide Web existed. In fact, people were doing all of those things long before the public Internet existed, using bulletin board software.

ICQ combines the best aspects of all of those technologies: the convenience of the e-mail message, the fun of IRC chatting, the power of the Usenet news posting, and the old bulletin board software's capability to determine which of your friends are online. This is how instant messaging was born.

 I've heard of instant messaging. What exactly is it?

An instant message is a way to say, "Hey, pay attention to me this very instant!"

Send a message to someone who you know is online and they will see your message the instant you send it. Unlike e-mail, where you have no idea whether the recipient is checking his e-mail, instant messengers let you keep track of the online status of the people with whom you regularly communicate. You can send messages and chat with someone when you see that they have come online, or you can send messages to them even though they are offline. Friends and associates can alert you to their specific status, such as, "I am connected, but away from my computer." Knowing when someone is online and available to communicate with you is what makes instant messaging so powerful.

America Online, one of the larger Internet access companies, has an instant messenger program simply known as AOL Instant Messenger. You can install this instant messenger by downloading it from AOL's Web site. Also, it comes installed with recent versions of Netscape Communicator.

Never wanting to be left out of a good thing, Microsoft has also entered into the instant messaging market with its MSN Messenger Service. Microsoft has been around a long time and has learned the importance of making its software work well with other software. MSN Messenger can be used to communicate with people using AOL Instant Messenger, at least in a limited fashion. MSN Messenger cannot find new AOL Instant Messenger contacts by searching the AOL database. You must either know the AOL contact nickname or have AOL installed so that you can find it. After you add a new contact to AOL Instant Messenger, you can access it from MSN Messenger Service.

ICQ, first an instant messaging program, was the model for these other programs. ICQ has grown into much more than an instant messenger, though. Although some of the instant messaging features in the AOL and MSN programs are nice, and in some cases are easier to use than ICQ, you sacrifice many other features that ICQ has to offer. Neither the MSN nor the AOL instant messaging program communicates with ICQ.

You can run more than one instant messaging software program simultaneously. Until instant messaging programs can truly communicate with one another in the same way most other Internet programs do, you have three options:

▶ Accept that some of your friends use a different instant messenger

▶ Convince your friends who don't use ICQ to start using ICQ

▶ Run more than one instant messenger program on your computer

How is ICQ different from AOL Instant Messenger?

You might have heard that AOL bought ICQ. This is true, but ICQ and AOL Instant Messenger have remained two distinct programs. AOL Instant Messenger enables you to send and receive messages and keep people in your Contact List in much the same way as ICQ. Where the programs differ is that ICQ has many more features than AOL Instant Messenger (and any of the other instant messenger programs).

AOL Instant Messenger is just that—a messenger—whereas ICQ has features such as the following:

▶ Instant messaging with eight different levels of online status

▶ Real-time chat

▶ File transfer

▶ Integration with the Web, including a personal homepage and a Web search

▶ Community-building tools that provide broadcast messaging and news posting

▶ E-mail capabilities

▶ Voice messaging

▶ Personal time management tools

Many of the ICQ features are available to you even when you are not connected to the Internet. Conversely, AOL Instant Messenger can't be launched when you aren't connected to the Internet, with the exception of a Preferences window.

Putting ICQ on Your Computer

ICQ is just like any other software. You have to find it, get it, install it, run it, and personalize it. This process is not difficult, but we will help you to avoid any pitfalls you might encounter.

Q4 How do I find ICQ?

We have made finding ICQ simple. There are only four officially supported sites: CNET, ZDNet, TUCOWS, and the ICQ FTP site. You should stick to one of these sites when considering a download site. Where you actually download ICQ is a matter of personal choice, although we recommend that you should not trust sites other than the ones we have listed, because other sites might have older, out-of-date versions or, possibly, files that contain viruses. Other download sites, such as Jumbo! (**www.jumbo.com**), have ICQ add-on programs. Feel free to download the ICQ add-on programs there, but stick to one of the official sites for the ICQ program itself.

CNET has a service called Download.com. This happens to be one of our favorite places to find free and shareware software. Using your Web browser, go to **www.download.com.** If you are visiting the Download.com site from a PC (not a Macintosh), the download choices for PCs are selected. If you wish to choose selections for a different type of computer, click the link that represents the type of computer on which you want to run ICQ. ICQ is currently available for the PC, the Mac, handheld computers running Windows CE, and any computer running Java.

From CNET's Download.com, choose Internet. On the next page of selections, choose Communications. You will see a list of communications software. Scroll down until you find the version of ICQ you want to install. Many versions of ICQ are available, depending on the computer and operating system (OS) you are running.

TIP

If you are running Windows 95, Windows 98, or Windows 2000, then look for a version of ICQ that is labeled version 99b or later. You can find the most current versions on the ICQ Web site, **www.icq.com**.

If you prefer ZDNet for your downloads, you will find ICQ at the top of its 50 Most Popular Free Files list. Find ZDNet at **www.zdnet.com**.

TUCOWS (The Ultimate Collection Of Winsock Software), **www.tucows.com**, was one of the very first Internet shareware download sites. It has grown into one of the largest repositories of software in the world. On the TUCOWS homepage, enter ICQ into its Quick Search. Also, specify what OS you are running. The ICQ program will come up in the results page. Click Download Now. You then are asked where in the world you are located so that TUCOWS can help you choose a download location closest to you for fastest download times. You again get to specify your location by choosing a site close to you. Some places have faster connections and databases of software that are updated more regularly. These are noted with colored check marks. Selecting this location automatically starts the download. If your Web browser isn't one of the newest ones, you might have to click the download link provided on the Web page.

A popular place to download the ICQ program is from the ICQ site itself (**www.ICQ.com**). The ICQ homepage is packed with lots of information. Look in the column to the far left of its Web page, entitled Free ICQ Software. Select the version of ICQ you want to download from this list of links. You will navigate to an ICQ download page, from which you can choose one of the other download sites or the ICQ FTP site. Don't worry if you know nothing about FTP. This capability is built into your Web browser, and clicking this link is similar to other types of Web downloads.

Whichever site you choose, once you have found the version of ICQ that you want to download, follow the directions on the site for downloading ICQ. The program tends to be large and can take 20 or 30 minutes to download over a 56Kbps modem. You are normally prompted for a place on your hard drive to store the ICQ program. You can store it in one of your Temp directories. The files you are downloading are the installation files. You don't need to create a special place to store these files. During installation, ICQ will create a directory on your hard drive in which to install itself.

TIP

Remember where you are saving the installation files. You will need to locate these files to begin the installation.

If you are disconnected for any reason while downloading the installation files, many of the newer Web browsers allow you to continue downloading where you left off, after you reconnect. Download accelerator programs also are available on some of the software download sites mentioned earlier. These programs enhance the speed of your download and usually have the ability to resume downloads if the download is interrupted.

Q5 Now that I have ICQ, how do I install it?

The ICQ file you downloaded from the Internet contains everything you need to run ICQ. In **Question 4**, which talked about downloading ICQ, we mentioned that you should make a note of where on your hard drive you saved this file. Well, it's time to use that now.

TIP

If you already have ICQ installed and you are installing a new version, then we highly recommend backing up your ICQ information. A free program called JVDE ICQ Backup will back up your files and save you from possible disaster. It's probably a good idea to back up your ICQ files regularly when you start using it. This free program is available on ZDNet, at **www.zdnet.com.**

Step-by-step installation

With Windows Explorer open, change to the directory in which you saved the downloaded file, and then follow these instructions:

1. Double-click the filename in **Explorer.** This launches the installation program.

2. Read every word of the **License Agreement.** If you think you can live with it, click the **Continue** button. Otherwise, click the **Exit Installation** button. Clicking **Continue** takes you to the next window.

3. Read the **License Note,** swearing that you read the license agreement on the previous page. At this point, you can agree to follow the license agreement, decline to follow it, or go back and read it again.

4. Assuming that you agreed to the license agreement, the next window that appears is the **Welcome** message. At this point, if you aren't already connected to the Internet, do so now. You do not have to exit the installation program while you are connecting. After you are connected, click the **Next** button.

5. Choose where on your hard drive you want ICQ installed. If you make no changes, the installation program installs ICQ in a directory appropriately named ICQ, created within the Program Files directory. Click **Next** after selecting the directory.

NOTE

When choosing where you want to install ICQ, you can also choose to install ICQ on a different hard drive or on a shared network drive. You might want to consult your network administrator before saving ICQ to a network drive.

6. The next window asks you whether it can add ICQ to the **Windows Start menu.** This is a good idea. Many times, you will need to start ICQ from the programs in the Start menu. Click the **Yes** radio button.

7. You are next asked to select a **ProgMan group,** an old term used before Windows had the year attached to the name. This is the name as it will appear in your Start menu. The installation chooses to call it ICQ. If you leave it this way, selecting **Start > Programs > ICQ** opens a list of ICQ program files. Leaving it as ICQ is probably fine, so click **Next.**

8. You now have the opportunity to customize ICQ to support other languages. If you are using Windows with no additional languages supported, click the radio button next to **I'm using an English System.** As the installation program notes, you can change this setting later. Click **Next.**

9. ICQ begins expanding and installing the program files. You might see a small window appear that contains the newly installed files. The next window you see tells you that the database needs to be compatible with the previous version of ICQ, and so forth. This is important only if you have a previously installed version of ICQ. It lets you know that the installation program is about to make changes to your currently installed ICQ, which means that you can't continue to use your old version. Assuming that this is not a problem for you, click **OK.**

ICQ should now be installed on your computer.

First-time Registrations

To begin using ICQ, you need to register with the ICQ server and obtain your **ICQ number.** This number is personal, unique and identifies you within the ICQ network. This number, distinctly yours, is not limited to the machine on which you have ICQ installed. It is possible to send and receive messages using your ICQ number on any machine where ICQ is installed.

After ICQ finishes installing, you are prompted to restart your computer. You will want to allow ICQ to restart your computer, making sure you have saved any of your work in other programs. Once your computer has restarted, launch ICQ for the first time by selecting it from your computer's Start menu. This automatically starts the ICQ Registration program which will walk you step-by-step through the registration process. If you are a new user, you need to get a number from the ICQ server before you can use the ICQ program.

Figure 1.2 shows the first of several windows in the ICQ registration process. In the top half of the window you are asked to select the type of connection you have with the Internet.

► **Modem (dial-up connection)**—Select this option if you are connecting to the Internet using your modem to dial using a telephone line.

► **Permanent (LAN, Cable Modem, etc.)**—Select this option if your computer is connected to the Internet through a local area network, or if you have installed a cable modem through your cable TV provider, or DSL through an Internet service provider.

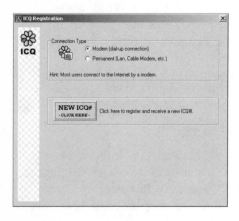

Figure 1.2 Begin registering by entering your Internet connection method.

Continue through the registration process by clicking the button on the bottom half of the window labeled, New ICQ# Click Here.

The next window in the ICQ registration process appears as shown in **Figure 1.3**. The information on the top half of this window is completely optional. You are not required to give personal information about yourself to ICQ or others in order to register ICQ. If you would like others to be able to find you through some of the ICQ search utilities you may want to enter your first and last names in the places provided. You can also enter an optional nickname. When others add you to their ICQ contact list, this is the nickname that will appear in their list.

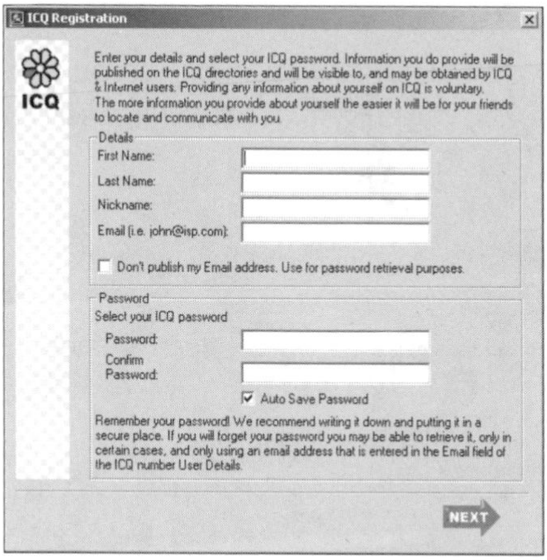

Figure 1.3 Enter only the optional identifying information you feel comfortable sharing with others.

Entering your e-mail address as part of the ICQ registration process is a good idea. This is the only mechanism ICQ has for verifying your identity in the event you lose your ICQ password. Losing your password without having registered your e-mail address could mean that you would lose any contact information you have stored in ICQ. If you are concerned about your personal privacy you can click the checkbox to signify that you don't want your e-mail address published to others.

Enter your password, twice for confirmation. The suggestion on the ICQ window is that you write your password down so you don't forget it. We would offer a different suggestion. Don't ever write down a password, for ICQ or any other program. Instead, choose a password that is easily remembered. It's even best if you can choose a different password for each application that requires you to enter a password. Because it isn't always possible to remember that many passwords, select one that does not have recognizable words, and some numbers. Click the Next arrow to continue to the next step in the ICQ registration, as shown in **Figure 1.4**.

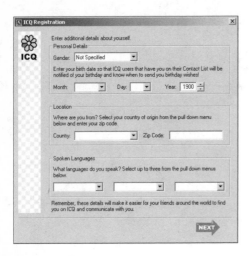

Figure 1.4 Personal information is fun to share with others.

Continuing on with the registration process you are prompted to enter your gender and birthdate. This optional information is fun to enter if you are looking for others to chat with that may be looking for someone of a particular age and gender. Also, entering your birthday will notify others who have you in their contact list of your birthday by sending them an ICQ reminder. It's nice to hear from lots of people on your birthday using this subtle reminder.

Entering a location will allow others to find people in their geographic location that might share similar interests. You can be general, and enter your country, or more specific by adding your postal ZIP code.

Entering the languages you speak will make it simpler for others to find you based on your ability to converse in the same language. You can specify only three languages. If you speak other languages, there are places in your personal information where you can make note of that so that others will learn what languages you speak. Also, make sure you can also write the language as well as speak it if you intend to use text messaging and chat.

Click the Next arrow to continue. At this point, your ICQ program will attempt to contact the ICQ server. If your connection information is improperly entered, or if you are not connected to the Internet while attempting to register ICQ, you will be shown an error message like the one shown in **Figure 1.5**. From this error message you can try to connect again, in case there was some random, temporary error in connecting. You can change your connection settings, or visit the ICQ troubleshooting page for more help.

Figure 1.5 You may need to configure your connection before continuing with your registration.

Once you have completed your registration, ICQ will inform you of your new ICQ number. You will not need to write it down as it will always appear at the top of your ICQ contact list window. It is a nice idea to include it in e-mail messages so that others can contact you.

In previous versions of ICQ, receiving your ICQ number marked the end of the registration process. With ICQ 2000a, there are still a few more steps. Notice in **Figure 1.6** that at the bottom of the window that has your new ICQ number, you are asked to choose some privacy and security settings.

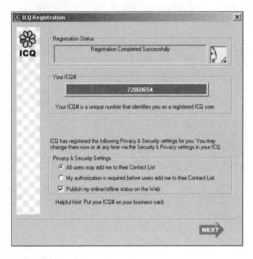

Figure 1.6 Once you have received your ICQ number you can set your privacy and security settings.

The privacy settings are very important. Allowing others to add you to their contact list without your permission means that they have complete access to the information stored in your user profile. If you want this information to remain fairly private, and released only when you give permission, you should uncheck the radio button labeled: All users may add me to their Contact List and select the option that requires your authorization.

If you want the world to know when you are either offline or online you can choose to have that status published on the Web. By unselecting this option, only people who have added you to their contact list will know your online status.

NOTE:

Changing your status to invisible mode will block everyone from knowing your online status.

The next step in the registration process launches the ICQ Services window (**Figure 1.7**). In this window you can select from several ICQ services:

▶ **Search for friends**—If you are setting up ICQ for the first time you may want to find out if some of your friends are also using ICQ.

▶ **Set the ICQ homepage as your browser's default start page**—If you don't already have your favorite page marked, you can always choose the ICQ page as your start page. This change is setup to be made by default. Unselect this if you don't want your browser's homepage changed.

▶ **Chat with a friend**—This option sets your status as available for chat. You are available for chat also when you are in online mode.

▶ **Subscribe to the ICQ newsletter**—You may choose to
receive news via e-mail from ICQ on a regular basis. You can
always unsubscribe any time you like by visiting the ICQ
homepage. You'll be notified when your subscription request
has succeeded as shown in **Figure 1.8**.

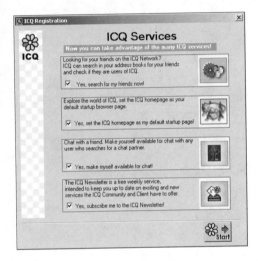

Figure 1.7 Choose ICQ services being careful to unselect the ICQ homepage
option if you don't want your browser's homepage to change.

Figure 1.8 ICQ will notify when each of your service requests has completed
successfully.

When you have completed your registration the ICQ Contact List will launch. An additional informational window also launches and closes automatically after a few seconds. This window will launch each time you launch ICQ and inform you of any new cool features.

Clicking on the **System Message,** as shown in **Figure** 1.9, you will receive your first ICQ message.

Figure 1.9 The new ICQ Contact List launches with no contacts, only your first ICQ message from the ICQ system.

The ICQ contact list will contain no contacts at this time. You are now ready to start adding contacts, sending messages and chatting with others. You may want to begin by clicking the ICQ button on your contact list and reviewing the menu. This is simple mode. We will cover switching to advanced mode later in the book.

What if I've forgotten my password?

If you have forgotten your password, follow these steps to have it sent to you by e-mail. This is the only method for obtaining your password.

1. Start a Web browser and go to **www.icq.com/password/**.

2. Enter your ICQ number, and you will receive your password in your e-mail. Remember that you will receive this password at the e-mail address you entered during your previous ICQ registration.

If you are unable to obtain your password, you have to reregister and obtain a new ICQ number. People who have you in their **Contact List** will not be able to contact you at the old ICQ number. You will have to contact each of them, giving them your new ICQ number.

To complete your registration, enter your ICQ number and password and click Next. Confirm your **Outgoing E-mail Server,** and again click Next. You have completed the Registration Window for an existing ICQ number, so click **Done.** The ICQ communicator program will launch automatically and your Contact List will appear.

What is the purpose of the For Admin Use button?

The setting on this button tells ICQ how to connect to the ICQ server. Unless you are given instructions by your system administrator, you should not change any of the settings. Changing these settings might make it impossible for the ICQ program to contact the ICQ server. Without the ability to contact the server, your ICQ program will not operate correctly.

I'm stuck behind a firewall. Now what do I do?

If you are installing ICQ on a company computer, it's possible that your company protects its computers with a piece of equipment called a *firewall*. Firewalls protect computers on your local area network (LAN) by acting as a barrier between computers on your LAN and computers on the Internet. You will need information from your network administrator about how to configure ICQ so that it can communicate through the firewall. Your network, if it is connected to the Internet, will use software known as a proxy server. *Proxy servers* route all the traffic from computers on a network behind a firewall to the Internet.

NOTE

Some proxy servers are configured to use a feature known as Winsock proxy. If your computer is configured to use Winsock proxy, you will not need to configure the firewall settings in ICQ.

To configure the firewall/proxy server settings in your ICQ program:

1. Click the ICQ menu and select **Preferences.**

2. The **Owner Preferences** window appears with a menu on the left side of the window. Select Connections.

3. In the **Connections Window General tab,** under **Connection Type,** select **Permanent** (LAN, Cable Modem, etc.).

4. Select the **Server Tab** and select the radio button, **Using Firewall.** Chances are good that you are also using a Proxy. **Select Using Proxy** and select the type of proxy from the drop down list. You may need assistance from your network administrator in this and the next step.

5. Select the **Firewall** tab to configure ICQ to operate behind a proxy or firewall.

Getting Cozy with ICQ

ICQ has many features, so it's a good idea to become comfortable with some of the most basic concepts. The most important and basic thing you need to know is your ICQ number. With this number, you have access to the many other facilities, many of which are not part of the ICQ software itself.

Q7   What's my address?

When you first start ICQ and use the wizard to install and request your ICQ number, your new number is displayed in the dialog box. Unlike your password, which you have to save in a place where you can easily find it, your ICQ number is always displayed for you whenever the ICQ window is displayed. Look in the upper-left corner of the ICQ window to see your number, as shown in **Figure 1.10**.

Figure 1.10 Your ICQ number is displayed at the top of your ICQ window.

How can I protect my children from objectionable material?

One of a parent's greatest fears about their child's use of the Internet is that they will be exposed to all sorts of nastiness. There are no guarantees that this won't happen. However, a parent can take responsible steps to limit this exposure. Whereas the Web has its Net Nanny and SurfWatch, ICQ has its **Words List** of objectionable words. The Words List feature checks all the incoming events, such as messages, user information, and chat requests, looking for words that you have entered in the list of objectionable words. By the way, this list is password-protected so that kids can't sneak in and change it.

The Words List feature is versatile. You can choose to block only the objectionable word, replacing the word with a character of your choice, or to block the entire event so that messages containing the offending language never appear.

To launch the Words List feature of ICQ, follow these steps:

1. Click the ICQ button.
2. Click **Security & Privacy**.
3. Select the last tab, called **Words List**, as shown in **Figure 1.11**.
4. Unlock the feature by entering your password. Click the **Unlock (Enter Protection Password)** button.

Figure 1.11 Protect young ones and yourself from unwanted objectionable material.

In the Words List dialog box, you will see the list of words that you have specified as objectionable (see **Figure 1.12**). You can add new words, edit the words that are there, or remove words from the list. If your idea of a good time isn't sitting around the old computer thinking of objectionable words to add to the list, you can choose to download a prepared list.

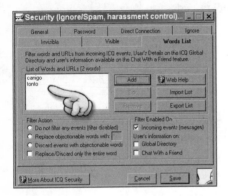

Figure 1.12 Enter your own objectionable words or import a list.

Clicking the Get Words List button takes you to the ICQ Web page that describes the Words List in complete detail.

Now, choose what you want ICQ to do when it encounters a word from your list:

▶ **Do Not Filter Any Events (Filter Disabled)**—The Words List will not check for any word.

▶ **Replace objectionable words with: ***—The Words List will search for words and replace them with *; you can change the * for another symbol, letter, or number.

▶ **Discard events with objectionable words**—All the events that contain a word from your list will never appear.

If you check the box in the last option, called Replace/Discard only the entire word, then when your objectionable word is actually an innocent part of a larger word, it will be considered objectionable only when the word appears alone. Examples of innocent words that might contain objectionable words are *cocktail* and *cockatiel.* Be careful when specifying words that also have both innocent and objectionable meanings, such as the word that is synonymous with *rooster.*

Q8 What do I get with my ICQ registration?

Few, if any, resources on the Internet give you as many features as ICQ. Now that your ICQ program is installed and configured, you are ready to start exploring the many ICQ features, including the following:

▶ Unlimited number of ICQ addresses

▶ E-mail address at ICQ.com

▶ E-mail software

▶ Web pages

▶ Personal homepage

▶ Instant messaging

▶ Chat software

▶ ActiveList participation

▶ Listing in the ICQ White Pages

ICQ has no current limit on the number of ICQ addresses a single user can have. You can choose to maintain different ICQ addresses. You could have an ICQ address that you use primarily for business, allowing business associates to see information such as your telephone number, e-mail address, and mailing address. ICQ is an excellent business tool. If you have your company information entered into ICQ, you can even provide a map to your company's building location. Your personal ICQ address can include information such as your hobbies, interests, or even romantic interests. You can choose to have a third ICQ address that you use primarily to communicate anonymously with others.

Companies, anxious for your Internet attention, are offering free, permanent e-mail addresses. ICQ began working with one such company, Bigfoot, to create a special version of ICQ just for Bigfoot users. Now, ICQ has begun offering its own free e-mail addresses and has included features that allow your ICQ program to be alerted when e-mail arrives.

ICQ, rather than replacing traditional e-mail with instant messaging, has created a program that works seamlessly with your normal e-mail. The ICQ program includes a full-featured e-mail program that enables you to compose, send, and receive e-mail.

Not only can you send and receive e-mail using the ICQ e-mail program, others can send messages to your ICQ program without having the ICQ program installed, by sending an e-mail message to you at your special ICQ pager address (**ICQ number@pager.ICQ.com**). The ICQ pager is not the only way that people without the ICQ program can communicate with you through ICQ. Your Web pager is a way others can communicate through the Web, sending messages to your ICQ program.

Speaking of the Web, ICQ enables you to have your own personal homepage, hosted right on your own computer. You can customize this page to offer information about yourself, while also offering a wide range of ICQ communication features to visitors of your page. If you already have a personal homepage, you can include the ICQ Personal Home Page panel in any Web page, turning the page into a full-blown ICQ communications center.

Of course, the reason most people install ICQ is for its Instant Messenger. Unlike other instant messengers, you can send messages to others regardless of their status, online or offline. If the person to whom you are sending a message is not online, the ICQ server can hold the message, delivering it as soon as they log in.

Aside from instant messaging, the ICQ chat software is unparalleled. ICQ has made the IrCQ version of the Internet Relay Chat program available to you separately from the ICQ program. You can include IrCQ chat in your own Web page, enabling others to chat right from your Web page.

Participation in ActiveLists is more than chat and more than instant messaging. By belonging to ActiveLists, you can send and receive messages to all the members of a group formed around a particular topic or interest. ActiveLists are virtual communities. For example, while we were writing this chapter, a 7.4 earthquake occurred in Mexico, just south of Mexico City, where we were working. Instantly, the members of our ActiveList began broadcasting messages to make sure we were safe. Unfortunately, soon after the quake, the phone lines went dead and we weren't able to answer for a few hours.

Section 1 Getting ICQ Happy

Your free listing in the ICQ White Pages might just surprise you someday when a long-lost friend or family member finds and contacts you using ICQ. Other Whitepages directories require that you find people using an address, phone number, or e-mail address. The ICQ White Pages enables people to find you through hobbies, associations, and past information.

Keep watching the ICQ homepage (**www.ICQ.com**) for new features as they are released. New things are added all the time. The ICQ homepage is also a great place to keep track of the most current version of ICQ. Until the day that ICQ starts charging for its program, you can download every new version for free.

Q9 ICQ looks difficult. Is there an easier way?

It's easy to get a little overwhelmed with all the features ICQ has to offer. If you primarily want to use ICQ to send and receive messages and chat with friends, you might want to hide some of the features. You can do this by using ICQ in Simple mode.

Changing to Simple mode does not change the way ICQ operates, nor does it limit what you are able to do in ICQ. You can choose to use advanced features whenever you like.

Switching between Simple and Advanced mode is easy. Click the ICQ button to bring up the menu. If you are in **Simple** mode already, your menu selection reads **Advanced Features.** If you are in **Advanced** mode, the menu reads **Simple (Basic Features).** Clicking either of these menu selections brings up the **Simple/Advanced Mode Selection dialog box,** shown in **Figure 1.13**, which tells you the mode you are in, and lets you switch to the other mode by clicking either the Switch to Simple Mode button or the Switch to Advanced Mode button. Only one button is active, based on which mode ICQ currently is in.

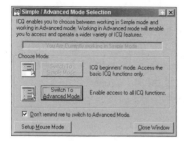

Figure 1.13 Switch between the Simple and Advanced modes to change what features are presented in the menus.

This dialog box also includes a button that enables you to choose which mouse button you want to use to bring up menus. **Question 10** explains how to add people to your Contact List. Once they have been added, you can access a menu by clicking a person's contact name.

Q10 How do I add people to my Contact List?

Adding people to your Contact List is easy, but can be a little confusing, because the folks at ICQ use the term "Users" to refer not only to you but also the people who use your ICQ software and the people you want to add to your Contact List. To add people to your Contact List, either use the **Add Users** button that appears on the ICQ window or click the ICQ menu, go to **Find/Add Users,** and then click **Find Users- Add To List.** Depending on which of these ways you decide to add users, a different window will appear.

A large Add Users button appears toward the bottom of the
ICQ window, as shown in **Figure 1.14,** which shows how the
button appears in Simple mode. If you are in Advanced mode,
the button appears in the same place, but on the left side of
the window. Clicking the Add Users button causes a new
window to appear on your screen, called Find/Add Users to
your list.

Figure 1.14 Click the Add Users button to add people to your Contact List.

The Add Users button launches the ability to search for people
you want to add to your Contact List. Find people by searching
based on their e-mail address, nickname, first name, last name,
or ICQ number. A **Search** button is provided after each category.
Click the Search button next to the information that you have
entered.

The Find/Add Users window is full of information. By selecting
the different tabs, you can contact many kinds of people, using
a wide variety of search and communication options in this
window. You will find features such as the following:

▶ The ICQ White Pages

▶ The ability to search other directories (ICQ LDAP search)

▶ Find chat with a friend

▶ Use the Invitation Wizard

▶ Get information about your four ICQ addresses

▶ Reach the world through ICQ International

▶ Share with people by using the Chat program

▶ Find resources for site building in the Webmaster Zone

▶ A place to express your feelings

▶ Use ICQ e-mail

▶ Configure the ICQ Telephony features

▶ Find others through Topic Directories

▶ Search the Web using ICQ Now!

▶ Get help or help others in the user participation area

The other way to add new users is by using the ICQ menu selection:

1. Click the ICQ button and select **Add/Invite Users.**

2. Click **Find User-Add To List.**

3. In the **ICQ Global Directory** dialog box, you are given a choice of user interfaces. Use the **Contact List Wizard** or choose to switch to the **Classic** mode by clicking the **Classic Mode** button in the bottom of the dialog box. You can also choose to use the ICQ White Pages to find contacts by clicking the **ICQ Whitepages** button in this dialog box.

Contact List Wizard

When you select Add/Invite Users, the default mode is the Contact List Wizard, shown in **Figure 1.15.** Using this wizard, you can begin your search by entering any of the following details:

▶ **Search by Email**—If you know the e-mail address of your contact, friend, or family member, ICQ will search its database for any matches containing the e-mail address you enter. Understand that this search criteria is very narrow, showing only the person whose ICQ registration contains that e-mail address. It's also quite possible that you might not find a match. Remember that entering an e-mail address is optional when registering. If your search does not bring up a match, ICQ will offer to send an e-mail message letting this person know that you are waiting for them on ICQ.

▶ **Search by Nickname**—If you know the nickname that your contact uses, enter it here. The search might bring up many people using that particular nickname. Look through the results list to see whether you can find the first or last name that matches the person you are looking for. If more than 40 names are returned in the result, the list will not be complete and you should narrow your search by entering a first or last name or both.

▶ **Search by First Name**—Type the first name of your contact to search for him or her. It is not a good idea to specify only a first name without specifying other search parameters. The search is too broad and will result in a list that is limited by the 40-name result limit.

▶ **Search by Last Name**—Type the last name of your contact. Combining the last name (or surname) with either the first name or nickname is your most likely chance of successfully finding someone registered on the ICQ network.

▶ **Search by Interest**—Find ICQ users with interests similar to your own.

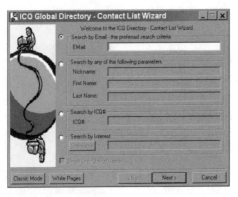

Figure 1.15 The ICQ Contact List Wizard is a powerful way to find people to add to your Contact List.

Classic mode

Clicking the Classic Mode button in the lower-left corner of the Contact List Wizard dialog box enables you to search in Classic mode. It's called Classic mode because earlier versions of ICQ used this mode, meaning that many people are comfortable with its look and feel. Classic mode is basically the same as Wizard mode, except for the layout. Wizard mode has radio buttons to choose your search method, whereas Classic mode has tabs.

ICQ White Pages search

The ICQ White Pages search is a very powerful search tool that lets you contact people based on a specific interest, location, age, or one of many other search criteria. The ICQ White Pages search is not necessarily a good way to find a specific friend or family member you hope to contact. It is much better for making new friends by searching based on a particular interest. Major search headings are provided, and by placing a check next to a heading, you can build detailed search criteria. If you are looking to find people who will communicate with you immediately, you can also limit your search to users that are currently online.

Depending on which mode you have selected, there are different methods of beginning your search. In the Wizard mode, you must click the Next button to start the search. In Classic mode and ICQ White Pages mode, click Search.

Remember, if more than forty people match your search criteria, a message window tells you that you should narrow your search. You still are allowed to see the first forty matches of ICQ users. The users are arranged by their ICQ number, so if your contact uses an old ICQ number, there is a greater chance of finding him in the list.

Once the ICQ White Pages Search has been completed, a list of names appears on the bottom of the ICQ White Pages Search Engine dialog box. Right-clicking a name from the list of results launches a menu from which you can do the following:

▶ Add to your Contact List

▶ Add to your Address Book

▶ See Users Details

▶ Send a message to this user

▶ View the ICQ user's homepage

After you find the person you want to add to your Contact List, click Next to add the contact to your list. Double-clicking on the contact's name will attempt to add the person to your Contact List.

When you add people to your Contact List who don't require that you first obtain their authorization to know when they are online, a message pops up telling you that the contact has been added to your Contact List and that the ICQ server will alert you when your contact is online. Otherwise, you must request their authorization and wait until you are authorized to see when that user is online.

You can arrange your list into groups, such as family, friends, co-workers, or any group you want to create. By clicking the User tab of your Contact List, you can view and manage the members of your group. Clicking the arrow next to the group expands the group. The default groups are as follows:

Groups

Manage groups by clicking on the name of any group, bringing up the following menu:

▶ **Create New Groups**—You can create as many groups as you need.

▶ **Close All Groups**—Contracts all the groups so that you see only the names of the groups.

▶ **Open All Groups**—Expands all the groups, enabling you to see every contact in every group.

▶ **Find Users**—Searches for a contact within your Contact List.

▶ **Separator**—On or Off. Choose whether you want to have a separator appear between your contacts who are online and those who are offline.

▶ **Group Mode**—Two types of Group modes are available. Select a Group mode depending on how you want your contacts to appear in the list. Group mode 1 displays all the names together. Group mode 2 separates online and offline users, with online users on top and offline users on bottom. In Group mode 2, group names appear twice in your Contact List.

▶ **Sort**—You can sort contacts either alphabetically or by online status, or you can leave them unsorted.

▶ **Contact List Tabs**—On or Off. Choose whether you want to view or hide the tabs at the top of your Contact List.

▶ **Show Extra Icons**—Choose whether you want to view or hide the icons that are shown after your contact's name.

Groups do not necessarily have to contain members. All of the options listed above are available to manage groups, with or without members. Groups that have members have three additional menu options:

▶ **Send Messages To**—Send a message to the entire group or to a specific member.

▶ **Send URLs To**—Send a URL to the entire group or to a specific member.

▶ **Send E-mail To**—Send e-mail to the entire group or to a specific member.

You can choose to add a contact to a particular group at any time by left-clicking the contact's nickname and choosing the Move To Group option from the menu.

Viewing user details

After you add people to your Contact List, you can choose to view their details whenever you want—they do not need to be connected to the Internet. Putting them on your Contact List stores a copy of their information on your computer. To view user details, follow these steps:

1. Click the nickname entry in your **Contact List** to bring up the menu.

2. Select **User's Details** from the menu.

3. View different information by clicking each of the tabs.

4. Click the **Done** button when you are finished viewing the user's information.

When viewing the user's information, you can also choose to save this information as a vCard. Click the **Save as vCard** button. You are prompted to save the vCard as a file on your hard drive. You might want to create a special folder on your hard drive for saving vCards. vCard files saved from ICQ will have the filename: ICQ#*[ICQ Number]*.VCF.

You can choose to keep this filename or create one that is more meaningful to you.

I have too many people named "John" in my list. How can I rename them?

Everyone gives a few moments of thought when they create their nicknames. If someone thinks that a particular nickname is cute, chances are good that many others have already thought so, too. As an old saying goes, "If you're one in a million, there are fourteen of you in Los Angeles." Nicknames aren't required to be unique on the ICQ network. It's quite possible that hundreds, maybe even thousands, of people using ICQ have chosen the nickname John.

Because it's possible to have confusing or duplicate nicknames in your Contact List, ICQ enables you to give these contacts more meaningful names. Of course, these names are changed only within your ICQ.

Click the contact you want to rename, which opens the **Send** menu. Select **Rename** from the menu. The menu disappears, and the contact nickname appears highlighted so that you can edit it. After you make your changes, click outside the ICQ window, and the changes will be saved.

 Why do some people appear in my Contact List as soon as I add them, whereas others require authorization first?

Just as you could choose whether or not people could add you to their Contact Lists without your authorization, others can make the same security choice. When you don't require their authorization to add them in your Contact List, their nicknames show up automatically in your Contact List. But when you attempt to add someone to your Contact List who requires authorization, a bit more work is necessary.

When trying to add someone who requires authorization, a
message window pops up, telling you that you can't add this
contact without being authorized. In this window, shown in
Figure 1.16, you can enter the reason why you want to add
him/her to your Contact List. You don't really need to write
anything, but it's nice for your contact if you give a little more
information about yourself or let them know why you want to
add them. (Of course, stalkers will never give the true reason.)
After you are ready, click **Request.**

Figure 1.16 Write the reason why you want to add this person to your
Contact List.

Your contact is now on your list, but you won't be able to see
his status until he authorizes you. The contact appears at the
bottom of your Contact List in a section called Awaiting
Authorization, as shown in **Figure 1.17**. While you are awaiting
authorization, you can still do the following:

▶ Send messages to the contact

▶ Swap e-mail with the contact

▶ See your history together

▶ Re-request authorization

▶ See your contact's homepage

▶ Inspect the user's details

▶ Rename your contact

▶ Delete the contact

▶ Customize the Alert/Accept mode for this contact

Figure 1.17 This is how your Contact List looks when you are waiting for authorization to add a user.

When your contact authorizes you, you receive a message letting you know that the user has accepted your request to add him to your Contact List. In this message, you can see his nickname, ICQ number, and e-mail address, as well as the date and time you were authorized to add him to your Contact List. You can also view his information and message history. When you're finished, click Close.

Finally, after you close the message, another message window opens to inform you that the user has been added to your Contact List. After you click OK in this message, your contact appears as a regular contact on your list. At this point, you can see whether the person is online or offline by the icon that appears next to the contact's name.

 I already have an old copy of ICQ. What happens to my contacts when I install the new version?

Your ICQ contacts are stored in your ICQ program's database. This database keeps track of many types of information important to ICQ. It's common for new versions of ICQ to make changes to this database, making older versions of the database obsolete.

Fortunately, the programmers at ICQ realize that people need to keep their contacts when installing a new version of ICQ. To meet this need, they created the **ICQ Database Converter.** During the installation of a new version of ICQ, you will be prompted to convert the existing database. In most cases, this is not a choice but more of an alert that your database is being converted. At this point, the ICQ Database Converter updates the structure of the database by reformatting the contact information you already have stored there. In the event that you need to run the ICQ Database Converter outside of the installation process, you can find this program in the ICQ folder of your Windows Start menu.

I am nervous about losing my contacts. How can I back up my ICQ database?

To be extra safe when upgrading, you might want to make a backup copy of your current ICQ database. Several ICQ backup utilities are available from software download sites on the Internet. We have tested many of them and found that several either don't work well or are difficult to use. You are welcome to experiment with one of these programs. You can find them on sites such as Jumbo!, Download.com, and TUCOWS.

If you want a more direct way to back up your ICQ database, find the ICQ folder by using Windows Explorer. The ICQ folder is most likely located beneath the Program Files folder. Viewing the ICQ folder in Windows Explorer will show you folders beginning with the name Db (for example, Db98b and DbNew). These are the directories that contain your ICQ database. Copy these folders to a new location on your hard drive, outside the ICQ folder.

When installing a new version of ICQ, the ICQ Database Converter likely will ask you which databases you want to update. There is one database per ICQ number registered in your ICQ program. The ICQ DataBase Converter will convert only databases for ICQ numbers already registered on your machine.

What happens if something goes wrong with my database conversion?

If something goes wrong with the conversion of your ICQ database or the Database Converter does not convert your files, don't bother clicking Help, because no information is available on how to resolve problems with database conversion.

Sometimes, the problem might be that the ICQ number you want to convert is not registered in your ICQ. This can happen when you want to add a database from another computer. Check your ICQ to make sure that each of the ICQ numbers you want to be converted are registered. Review the list of ICQ numbers that your ICQ Database Converter believes are registered. If the database you want to be converted is not found there, close the Database Converter and follow the directions for registering an existing ICQ user, which are found in the section "Registration for Existing Users" under **Question 5**.

If you experience problems with your database conversion, your best bet is to seek help from other ICQ users. Here's one way to locate help provided by other users:

1. Click the **Add Users** button. This might seem contrary to common sense, but trust us at this point.

2. From the **Find/Add Users to your list** dialog box, select the User Participation tab.

3. Click the **User to User Help** selection in the first column of selections. This will launch a Web page listing User to User Voluntary help Web sites.

From this page, you can visit chat sites specifically for help, read frequently asked questions (FAQ) pages, or visit some of the help desk pages created by ICQ users.

Finding Family and Friends

Q14 Can I send ICQ to my cousin?

There are millions of ICQ users currently, and many more millions will be on the ICQ network soon. One of the fastest ways that ICQ has grown has been through invitations from its members to others. Even though others aren't required to have the ICQ software to communicate with you, getting your friends to install ICQ means you can see when they are online and can share many of the more advanced communication features of ICQ.

You can certainly give people the simple ICQ Web page address, **www.icq.com**, and tell them to download the software. However, it's much easier for them to use an ICQ Invitation from you to join ICQ. From the ICQ menu select **Add/Invite Users** and then click **Invitation to join ICQ.** You are given three choices for letting ICQ know who you want to invite. Choose **Search address books on my computer.** This option searches through address books that you might have stored in your e-mail programs and builds a list of everyone you have in your Contact Lists. You can then select to send them an invitation by checking the check box next to each name. When you have checked everyone you want to invite, you can also add a personalized message to be included with the ICQ default invitation. This is probably a good idea. People today receive so much unsolicited e-mail that they might choose to ignore a message that does not immediately appear personal.

Invite your friends by clicking on the **Invite a friend** button. This choice is similar to the first choice, except you are asked to enter the person's e-mail address. If you don't know the e-mail address of the person you want to invite, you can search through several Internet-based directories by clicking the **Search User's e-mail in other directories** button. This is a little confusing, because clicking this button enables you to search through directories by both the person's e-mail address and name. If you have someone's e-mail address and don't know the person's name, this is a way you might be able to find it.

The third choice enables you to search for people using LDAP (see the sidebar "LDAP" under **Question 15**).

Q15 I lost my friend's ICQ number. How can I find him?

If your friend has ever had an ICQ number, then chances are good that his information can still be found in the ICQ server. The Add/Invite Users tool enables you to look for your friend by using his e-mail address, ICQ nickname, or first and last names. If your friend has a common name, searching by first and last name is a difficult prospect, because the ICQ server returns only the first forty names in its database. In fact, the server warns you that your search has returned too many matches and that you should narrow your search.

ICQ White Pages

The **ICQ White Pages Search Engine** lets you find people by specifying not only their e-mail address, but all types of personal, identifying information, including the following categories (see **Figure 1.18**):

▶ **Name & Email**—You can choose to enter the first name, last name, or e-mail address, or all of these. If you met the love of your life and only know their first name, where they work, and their approximate age, you might try entering just the first name in this category.

▶ **Age, Gender, Language**—This category is useful only if you have other information, such as the person's name. This category is good for narrowing a search that yields too many results. Age is entered as an age range, so you don't have to know the person's exact age. Knowing whether they are a man or woman also might help you narrow your search. You can narrow your search even further by specifying what language the person speaks.

▶ **Location**—One of the best ways to limit your search is to enter a city, a state, or even a country. Entering only a city can be confusing if the city has a generic name like Springfield, because many cities are named Springfield.

▶ **Occupation & Company**—Great for finding old friends from work or even new job prospects.

▶ **Interests**—ICQ gives its users the power to find people based on criteria such as what hobbies you like, what sports you watch or play, your favorite rock stars, or your favorite cartoon characters.

▶ **Past Information**—Finding someone from a long time ago can be frustrating if they've changed e-mail addresses, gotten married and changed names, or switched employers. Entering your past information makes it much easier for people to find you.

▶ **Affiliation/Organization**—Entering your associations with professional societies, charitable organizations, political action groups, or social clubs is one more way to find people who share your life's interests.

▶ **Homepage**—You put a lot of work and heart into that homepage, so you might as well let people take a look. Also, because ICQ doesn't really have a place to enter pictures of your kids and pets, your homepage is the perfect place.

It's important to remember that when searching in any of these categories, your search is limited to only those people who have entered information in that category. For example, if you are looking for Joe Jones from Springfield, Massachusetts, and you also include that he is 18-22 years old and speaks English, you might not find the Joe Jones you are looking for if he hasn't entered the language that he speaks.

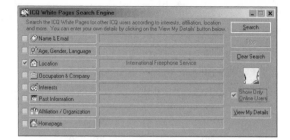

Figure 1.18 The ICQ White Pages can find people by interest, hobby, or past information.

The **Past Information** field can be useful if you have a person's old e-mail address, know what school she once attended, or know the branch of the military she once served in. Finding a match in any of these categories depends solely on the information the person you are looking for has chosen to enter.

LDAP

You're probably familiar with Web page directories on the Internet. Without them, no one could find what he is looking for. Not long after Web page directories were created, directories of people began springing up. Colleges and universities began maintaining student and faculty directories, and many companies began listing employee directories on the Internet. Eventually, "Whitepages" directories were created on the Internet, enabling people to list their e-mail addresses and other contact information so that others could contact them.

As these directories were formed, no standard way of storing information existed. This made it nearly impossible for software programs such as ICQ to query these directories. A standard was needed. Out of this need grew the x.500 standard. If you think the name sounds scary, so is the standard. A lightweight version of x.500 called LDAP, or *Lightweight Directory Access Protocol,* was created to provide a standard way of storing and retrieving Whitepages information. Programs that store Whitepages information are called LDAP servers.

Today, thousands of LDAP servers are on the Internet. Schools, companies, and public Whitepages directories use LDAP servers to manage their contact information. ICQ has several LDAP servers entered in its LDAP search capabilities. These servers, named Bigfoot, InfoSpace, InfoSpace Business, Switchboard, and WhoWhere, can help you find people when the ICQ directory fails to locate the person you are looking for, either because too many matches are returned or because the person has not chosen to enter her name or e-mail address into the ICQ database.

 How do I know whether I've found the right person?

If you think that you or your friend's name is unique, you're probably wrong. Only people like Moon Unit Zappa have truly unique names. When you do a search in ICQ to find a person, check the user's information to see whether it matches what you know about the person you are trying to contact.

One thing specifically you can check in the user's information is the e-mail address. Many people will add their e-mail addresses even if they have not entered any other information. With the e-mail address, you can search in directories such as the ICQ White Pages or Bigfoot to find a match. Another place to search is in the Yahoo! People search (**http://people.yahoo.com/**). This Yahoo! service, formerly known as Four11, has a gigantic database of people and their e-mail addresses.

You can use the Bigfoot LDAP search from within ICQ by clicking the ICQ menu, selecting the Invitation Wizard, and choosing Search in other e-mail directories. Or, you can visit the Bigfoot homepage and search using the Bigfoot site, at **www.bigfoot.com/**.

If you aren't sure, you might try a polite inquiry to the person whose ICQ number you've found to see whether they are indeed the person you are trying to contact.

Connecting

Q17 How do I connect to the ICQ network?

Whenever you start the ICQ program, it attempts to contact the ICQ network. You must first be connected to the Internet for ICQ to log in to the ICQ server. If you are not connected to the Internet when you first start ICQ, it will let you know that it has failed to log in to the ICQ server and will switch itself into Disconnected mode. After you connect to the Internet, you have to instruct your ICQ program to connect to the ICQ network, by clicking the status box in the bottom of the ICQ window and selecting **Available/Connect.**

NOTE

If you have ICQ in your Startup folder, ICQ will launch each time you start or reboot your computer. If you use a modem to connect to the Internet, ICQ will launch before you are connected, and ICQ's attempt to connect to the ICQ server will fail.

Instead of having ICQ launch and fail every time you start or reboot your computer, you can use the **ICQ NetDetect Agent.** This little application starts when your computer starts, but it does not launch ICQ until you connect to the Internet. To turn on the ICQ NetDetect Agent, you should follow these steps:

1. Click the ICQ menu.
2. Go to **Preferences & Security.**
3. Click **Preferences.**
4. Once the Preference window is open, click the tab named **Connection.**
5. Check the last option box, **Launch ICQ on Startup.**

The next time you start your computer, you will see a yellow icon with the letters ICQ in your left tray. This means that ICQ is ready to run as soon it detects an Internet connection.

By double-clicking the icon, you will be able to open ICQ even if you don't have a connection. Also, right-clicking the icon causes the following list of options to appear:

▶ **Open ICQ**—Runs ICQ.

▶ **Edit Launch List**—ICQ NetDetect Agent runs the programs on this list after it detects an Internet connection.

▶ **Launch Application**—Appears only if you have an application in your Launch List other than ICQ. You can choose which application to run.

▶ **Disable or Enable**—ICQ NetDetect Agent will not run if there is a red circle around the ICQ letters and a red line crossing them. This means that the ICQ NetDetect Agent is Disabled.

▶ **What is this?**—Provides you information about the ICQ NetDetect Agent.

Launch Programs Automatically When You Connect

With the ICQ NetDetect Agent, you can launch programs (such as NetMeeting, CU-SeeMe, and IRC) and e-mail clients (such as Outlook or Eudora) whenever a network connection is established. Network connections are established by your computer whenever you connect to the Internet.

To have the NetDetect Agent launch these programs, you must edit the **NetDetect Agent Launch List**. Each program in the Launch List will be executed whenever a network connection is established. You can edit the Launch List by doing the following:

1. Right-click the **ICQ NetDetect Agent** icon found in your Windows tray. Remember that this icon is there only if ICQ is not running. To start the ICQ NetDetect Agent, select it from the ICQ folder of your Start menu and then click the NetDetect Agent icon in the tray.

2. From your ICQ Preferences window, click the **Connections** tab.

3. Click the **Edit Launch List** button. A window called **ICQ NetDetect Settings** will open.

4. Click the **Add** button. Another window appears, as shown in **Figure 1.19**, in which you have to enter the following information:

   —**Enter Application Name**—Type the name of the program you want to add to your Launch List. If you leave this blank, when you select the next option the default name of the application will be automatically filled in.

   —**Application Executable Path**—This is asking you for the location within your computer of the executable file (.exe extension) that you want the ICQ NetDetect Agent to launch. For example, if you want to run NetMeeting, your path might be something like this: C:/Program Files/Netmeeting/CONF.exe. The location of the executable file depends on where it was installed. If you have trouble finding the application, you can use the Browse button to look for it. Sometimes this is faster and easier than typing the entire path.

—**Command Line Parameters**—If your program is launched with special parameters, you can add them here. For example, you can add the name of a document you want Microsoft Word to open immediately when it is launched by adding the path and name of the document here.

—**StartUp Path**—Some programs require that they be started from a particular folder or directory so that certain files are available by default. When this is the case, enter the path to this directory or use the Browse button to locate it on your hard drive.

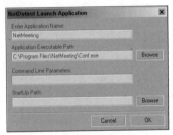

Figure 1.19 Enter the information to run the program with ICQ NetDetect Agent.

After you have the correct path, click OK. You are returned to the ICQ NetDetect Settings window, and you now should see the program you added with a checked box on the left side. If you uncheck the box, the program will not run. Every program that is checked will run every time a connection to the network is present.

When you finish adding all the programs you want to run, click OK. We recommend that you not add too many programs, because it will take a long time to load them and your computer might run out of memory.

CAUTION

With the ICQ NetDetect Agent, you can also open files, such as pictures and Word documents. The ICQ NetDetect Agent will open them fine when the connection is detected. But try closing them! They will keep opening in a continuous loop. The ICQ NetDetect Agent will not go away and will remain in your icon tray, detecting the connection every few seconds.

We recommend adding to your ICQ NetDetect Agent Launch List only those programs that you want to have launched when an Internet connection has been detected. The ICQ Net-Detect Agent works perfectly with this kind of program. Once the program is launched, the ICQ NetDetect Agent goes away and does not remain as an icon in your Windows tray.

What happens if ICQ won't connect?

Quite often, the ICQ network becomes unavailable and you are told by the program to try again in a few minutes. As the program suggests, keep trying for a while. If you are still having trouble, try manually selecting the **Offline/Disconnect** mode and then immediately trying to switch to **Online** mode. Sometimes this clears any problem that you might be having.

If you are still unable to connect, try shutting down the ICQ program by clicking the small *x* in the upper-right corner of the ICQ window. Restart ICQ by selecting the ICQ program from your Start menu. The ICQ program will reload, play the foghorn sound, and once again try to connect. If ICQ will still not connect, there are only two other possibilities. The first is that your computer's memory has become full, causing your ICQ program to not operate correctly. The only way to solve this problem is to reboot your computer, clearing the computer's memory and giving all the programs a fresh start. The second possibility is that the ICQ server is not available at this time; the only recommendation for this situation is to try again later.

Q18

I'm trying to finish writing a novel, but I have too many friends with ICQ interrupting me. How can I let people know that I don't want to be disturbed?

As an instant messenger, it's important for ICQ to be able to alert others to your current online status. When ICQ first loads, it connects to the ICQ network and switches from the Disconnected mode to Available/Connect mode. In this mode, you are available to receive messages and chat requests.

You can remain connected to the ICQ network and manually place your ICQ in a mode that blocks or discourages people from sending you messages. Let others know when you're away from your computer, don't want to be disturbed, or are ready to communicate and chat with others by changing the status. Click in the status box, as shown in **Figure 1.20**, and select one of the status modes listed here:

Figure 1.20 You can change status by clicking in the status box located at the bottom of the ICQ window.

▶ **Away**—Tells users that you are away from your desk. They can still leave you a message, and their Contact List entry will blink, notifying you that an incoming message has been received. The ICQ program automatically puts itself in Away mode if you have not typed on your keyboard for a specific length of time. You can set the length of time ICQ waits before putting itself in Away mode. By default, ICQ waits 10 minutes. You can enter Away mode manually by clicking the status display box in the bottom of the ICQ window and selecting Away from the popup menu.

▶ **Extended Away/NA**—Lets users know that you either have not been at your keyboard for a while or do not plan to be there. Like the Away mode, N/A can be set manually by clicking the status display in the bottom of the ICQ window and selecting N/A Extended Away from the popup menu. ICQ enters N/A mode automatically after you have been away from your keyboard for a specific length of time. Like Away mode, you can set the length of time ICQ waits before switching into N/A mode. By default, ICQ waits 20 minutes after your last keystroke before entering N/A mode automatically.

▶ **Occupied (Urgent Messages)**—Use this mode if you're online but working at your keyboard and don't want to be disturbed unless it's urgent. People can still send you messages, although they are prompted to send messages only if they are urgent. If people choose to send you messages while you are in Occupied mode, they are given the option of sending the message to your Contact List, in which case you will not get an audible alert. You will see a message icon next to the contact's name in your Contact List, letting you know that a message is waiting to be read. If the user chooses to send you the message in Urgent mode, then you will hear an audible alert, and the message will blink in your Contact List and task bar.

▶ **DND Do Not Disturb**—Use this mode if you're at your computer but under a deadline and don't even want to receive urgent messages. You don't want to shut down ICQ, because it's handy and you still want to get messages that you can review later. Users are given the option to send a message to your Contact List. You will not receive an audible alert when this message arrives. When you check your Contact List, you will see which contacts have sent you messages by the message icon that appears next to their name.

▶ **Available/Connect**—Lets your contacts know that you are online and available to receive messages, URLs, files, and chat requests. Unless you have changed your preferences to disable sounds, you are sent an audible alert when messages arrive. ICQ enters Online mode by default after connecting to the ICQ server. Users who send you messages will not receive any warning messages, as they did in the previously discussed status modes.

▶ **Free For Chat**—Normally, you are notified when one of your contacts wants to chat with you, and your permission to chat is requested. If you're feeling particularly chatty, or your business has integrated a support-by-chat feature into its Web page, you can choose the Free For Chat mode. Selecting this mode enables others who have you in their Contact Lists to know that you are accepting all chat requests. ICQ will automatically accept all requests to chat and start the Chat application.

▶ **Privacy (Invisible)**—For the ultimate in privacy, you can switch to Invisible mode. Once you set ICQ to Privacy mode, better known as Invisible mode, your online listing in Contact Lists will disappear. In this mode, people will not be able to send you messages, URLs, or chat requests.

▶ **Offline/Disconnect**—ICQ can work only when communicating with the server at ICQ.COM. When you are disconnected from the Internet, ICQ can't contact the server, and the program automatically enters Sleep mode, which includes setting the status to Offline. You can also manually switch to the Offline mode by clicking the status box at the bottom of the ICQ window and selecting Offline/Disconnect. You will appear offline to others and you can't send or receive instant messages, request chats, transfer files, or use any of the ICQ communications functions. You can think of this as the Off button for ICQ communications.

Is ICQ useful in Offline mode?

In Offline mode, you can still use features of ICQ that do not include communicating with the ICQ server. You can use the Web search, check the user information in your ICQ Contact List, and use many of the ICQ services, such as managing your To Do list, notes, reminders, e-mail, Phone-Follow Me, and the Message Archive.

Many of the features in the ICQ menu, accessible by clicking the ICQ button, are also available when disconnected. You can set any of your preferences and security features. About the only features in the ICQ menu not useable when disconnected are the Add/Invite Users and Invitation Wizards.

People who have you in their Contact Lists can choose to send messages to you through the ICQ server. Upon reconnecting to the ICQ server, any messages that were sent to the server while you were disconnected are waiting for you and are delivered to you as soon as you reconnect.

NOTE

When you are disconnected from the ICQ server, your personal ICQ homepage is no longer accessible.

We'd like to mention one last little thing about status. When you click the status box at the bottom of the ICQ window to bring up the menu, you will notice that the top menu selection is Random Chat. We realize that this is an odd place for this menu selection to appear. Random Chat is not an ICQ status. You will learn about the fun things you can do with the Random Chat feature in the "Chatting" portion of **Section 2.**

How come every time I come back from getting a snack, ICQ has changed to Away mode?

ICQ lets people who have you in their Contact List know when you've been away from the computer for at least 10 minutes. When no keystrokes have occurred on your computer for about 10 minutes, ICQ changes from Online to **Away** mode. After a while in Away mode, if you still haven't returned, ICQ changes automatically to **N/A (Not Available)** mode, also known as **Extended Away** mode.

This feature of ICQ keeps you from having to remember to set which mode you want to be in when you leave your computer.

How do I set the length of time ICQ waits before switching to Away or N/A mode automatically?

To change the length of time that you can be away from your computer before ICQ changes modes to Away mode or N/A mode, follow these steps:

1. Click the **ICQ menu** and select **Preferences.**

2. In the Owner Prefs For window, select the **Status Mode** option.

3. Change the time ICQ waits until changing to either the Away and/or N/A mode.

4. If you choose, you can rename the status. **Figure 1.21** shows the Away status renamed to Ignore. Renaming the status is only for your benefit. Anyone contacting you sees the standard status names. You can also choose to personalize the status message that the person trying to contact you sees when they try to send you a message. Notice that Online does not have a setting, because users will not see a message when contacting you in this mode.

5. Set the mode options in the lower half of the Status tab of the preferences window. Notice that these options do not change when selecting a different status from the drop-down list.

Table 1.3—Status Options

Mode	Description
In ICQ versions before ICQ 2000a Automatically Set "Away" When Screen Saver is Activated	If your computer is configured to have a screen saver start when you are away, the screen saver's activation will also cause ICQ to enter Away mode. If you have ICQ set to automatically enter Away mode in 10 minutes, and your screen saver set to appear in five minutes, ICQ will enter Away mode in five minutes.
Automatically Set Away After ?? Minutes of Not Using the Computer	This is where you can set the length of time you can be away from your keyboard before ICQ switches to Away mode. We say "keyboard" and not "computer" because the time is measured from the last time you've typed anything on the keyboard.

Mode	Description
Automatically Set N/A After ?? Minutes of Away	Set the number of minutes your computer is in Away mode before switching automatically to N/A mode. The length of time from your last keystroke to N/A mode is the length of time set in Away mode plus the length of time you set here. The minimum time is two minutes, and the maximum is 1,000 minutes (about 16 hours).
Show Messages in Tray in All Status Modes	When incoming messages are received when not in Online mode, checking this option alerts you of the incoming messages by displaying a small flashing icon in your computer's tray (usually the bar along the bottom of your screen).
Disable "Online Alert" Messages in "Away," "DND," "N/A," and "Occupied"	ICQ normally alerts you with an audible message or sound when your contacts come online. You can choose to disable these messages when in modes other than Online. If your computer is connected to the Internet on a dedicated connection (always connected), you might want to uncheck this to be alerted when contacts are online, even when you are not at your computer.

▶ Click the **Answering Service** button from the ICQuick bar on the right side of the ICQ contact list window.

▶ Select the status mode you want to customize by selecting it from the drop down list in the ICQ Answering Service window. (see **Figure 1.21**)

▶ You can select messages you would like displayed by selecting them from the second drop down list, or type in a custom message in the text box on the right. Rename the messages by clicking the **Rename Message Name** button beneath the drop down list.

▶ Set up special messages for your personal Web site visitors. (**Figure 1.21**) by typing the message into the **Outgoing Web Message** box.

▶ Click the **Save** button when finished.

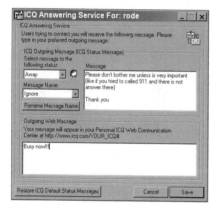

Figure 1.21 Customize your status messages and set automatic Away and N/A status times in the Status tab.

NOTE

When either Away or N/A mode is set automatically by ICQ, returning to your keyboard and typing or moving your mouse causes ICQ to return to Online mode. If you set Away or N/A mode manually, typing does not cause ICQ to switch back automatically.

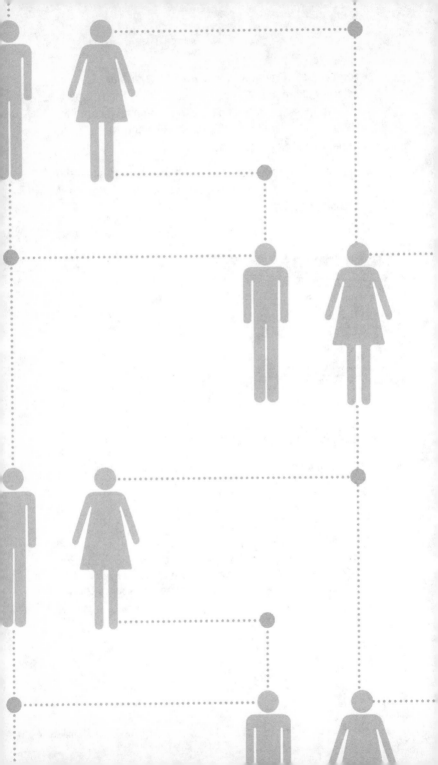

Section 2
Communicating

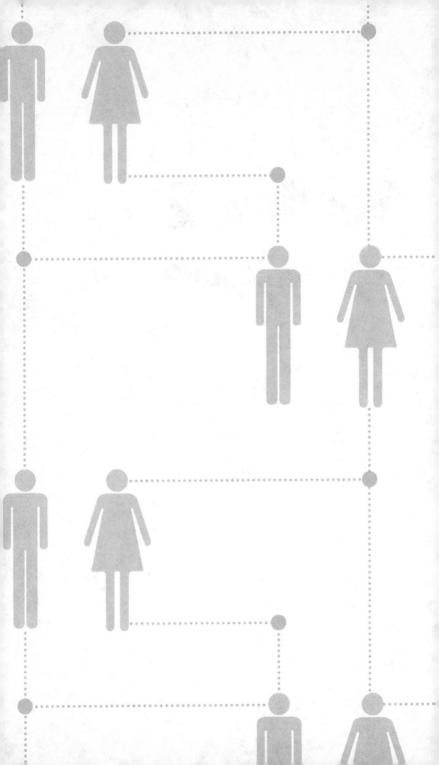

Communicating

Communicating has always been an important part of humanity. As social animals, humans like to express how they feel and, more specifically, ask for what they want. Even before verbal language, we communicated with signs. Fortunately, we have been evolving, and communication with other humans has greatly improved.

Interestingly, when e-mail fails or the computer crashes, we still rely on the telephone, a technology developed more than a hundred years ago, for communications. More than any other communications technology, the phone has changed the way we live and interact with one another. The introduction of radio and television earlier in the century began a trend toward static, one-way, mass communications. Our culture became redefined by what we heard on the radio or saw on television. No two-way communication technology could match that power; consequently, our lives, in many ways, became defined by the few people who control the mass media companies.

This type of control was true until the early part of this decade, when the government experiment in communications, DARPANet (Defense Advanced Research Projects Agency Network), became the public Internet. A revolution in communications occurred almost overnight. The world became a smaller place, and everyone on the planet became our neighbor. It's interesting to note that two considerable advancements in communications over the Internet were created in the tiny country of Israel: the Internet Phone—and now ICQ.

More than a new way to communicate, ICQ is an integrator of technologies into a single, powerful, communications utility. Messaging, e-mail, and electronic chat began in the 1980s with the birth of the personal computer. Thousands of people connected daily over modems using computers such as the Commodore 64, the Radio Shack TRS 80, and the IBM PC. Bulletin board systems, simply known as BBSs, enabled people in a local area to call into a single computer and interact in a network shaped like a star with a single hub. It wasn't a true network, because the computers had no real peer-to-peer communications capability. They were limited to what they could share through the computer running the BBS. Eventually, BBS computers found a way to call each other at night and relay messages, forming the first e-mail and computer-based electronic news distribution.

Exchanging messages, chatting, swapping voice messages, sending and receiving URLs, and file transfer are some of the options that ICQ provides for you to communicate with others. ICQ has all of these powerful communications features and the security of blocking communications from people with whom you'd rather not have contact.

Messaging

Messaging is the basic way to communicate through ICQ; therefore, it's the most used feature. Get instant messages from your friends and answer them in seconds. It's simple, fast, and easy to use. You can send as many messages as you want to as many people as you have in your Contact List.

 **I am all set up. How do I send an instant message?**

Once you're set up and contacts are in your list, the excitement starts. To send a message:

1. Look through your **Contact List** and find the person to whom you'd like to send a message. Click the contact, and a menu will appear.

2. Click the first option in the menu to send a message. The message window will pop up, ready for you to type your message.

3. After you type your message, click the **Send** button in the lower-left corner of the window.

When you see the animated ICQ icon faces moving, your message is in the process of being sent. When the message disappears, it means that your message was successfully sent.

In **Figure 2.1**, notice that the ICQ number, nickname, and e-mail address of your contact are displayed along the top of the message window. This is particularly useful if you are corresponding with more than one person at a time. It's possible, and sometimes common, to have several communication sessions going simultaneously. It can be fun trying to keep them all straight, and the information along the top of the message window becomes essential.

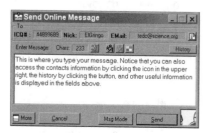

Figure 2.1 The message window has many features for displaying contact information.

It isn't necessary for you to be connected to the Internet or to the ICQ network when you construct your message. As soon as you connect to the Internet and the ICQ network, your message will be sent. Don't forget that you aren't connected and mistakenly think your message has been sent instantly.

TIP
A faster way to send a message is to double-click the nickname of the contact to whom you would like to send a message.

Sometimes, after you click the Send button, your message is not sent. In this case, a dialog box appears, letting you know that ICQ **Can't Send Online Message.** You are given a reason for the failure, such as Can't establish a DIRECT connection to user. You'll then be given four options:

▶ **Send Thru Server**—This means that your message will be sent to the ICQ server, and the server will act as an intermediary and send the message to your contact for you.

▶ **Auto-Send Later**—Your ICQ will keep the message in your outbox and it will try to send it later.

▶ **Retry**—Try to send your message again immediately.

▶ **Cancel**—This aborts your attempt to send the message and your message will be lost.

The bottom of the message window has a handy check box. By checking this box, events that can't be sent directly to a contact because a direct connection could not be established will automatically be sent through the ICQ server.

One of the first things you may notice when you start using ICQ is that your $100 keyboard sounds like a $10 typewriter. This is a feature, not a bug. Someone thought it would be cute to play the sound of an old typewriter as you send messages. Some people love this sound, but others hate it. The ICQ programmers, knowing that this nice touch could become a little bit annoying, give you the choice of turning this sound on or off. To do that, you can press the small icon with a speaker on it in the message window. If the icon appears with a red cross through it, the sound is turned off.

Sometimes, you may be writing a message to someone you've just met and need some topics of conversation. View the contact's information by clicking the small icon with the letter *i* in it. You will see the information icon in the upper-right corner of the message window, just after your contact's e-mail address. Click the icon, and a window with all the information your contact has chosen to enter will appear. This is also a great place to take notes about the contact while you are corresponding: "Likes artichokes; allergic to red wine." For more information on user information, see **Question 10**.

Individualize your messages. Take the extra time to send messages using something other than black letters on white background in Times Roman font. In the message window, you are also able to change the font type, style, size, and color, as well as the background color of the message.

Get creative by clicking the small icons above the area where you type your message:

▶ Choosing the first icon, three letter As all in black, pops up the option to change the font type, font style, and font size. You can also decorate your text with underline or strike-through.

▶ Clicking the second icon, the letter A in different sizes and colors, a list of colors will be displayed. Choose your text color from the list.

▶ The third icon, a colorful square, enables you to change the background color of the message window.

Your message will be sent with the font type, font style, font size, font color, and background color you choose. In case the recipient of your message does not have the font type you've chosen, the message will be displayed using the contact's default font. In most cases, the default font is Times New Roman.

In the ICQ 2000a version your message window can appear in either single message mode, the one most familiar to people who have used prior versions, and split message mode, which displays an ongoing dialog. Change display modes by clicking the **MsgMode** button in your Message window (See **Figure 2.1**).

Q21   Is there a limit to how much I can send in each message?

The size of the message you can send depends on the version of ICQ both you and your contact are running. You can type a maximum of 450 characters if the other person has an older version of ICQ (lower than 99a) or if your contact is offline. For newer versions, you can type as many characters as you want. There is a character counter in the message window. This counter is in the center just above where you write the message. This will alert you to the size of your message as you type.

If your contact is offline or has an older version, and you've exceeded the number of allowable characters, a window message will appear, allowing you to do the following:

▶ **Send Thru E-mail**—Send your message through e-mail. To use this feature, you had to first provide ICQ with your pop mail account. This is the name of the server that manages your e-mail account. The ICQ e-mail window will appear, and you may continue typing or choose to send it by clicking the Send button.

▶ **Auto-Send Later**—Your message will be kept in the outbox folder and ICQ will attempt to send it later.

▶ **Edit**—This option will take you to the original message, where you can shorten your message.

▶ **Cancel**—This aborts your message.

So, in some cases, the limit is your creativity or the time you can spend writing a message. Just remember that ICQ is an instant messenger, and there are some things that e-mail is more appropriate for.

 **My friends aren't online right now. Can I still send them a message?**

With ICQ, you can send messages even when your friends are offline. Follow the directions for sending messages given in **Question 20**. Sending a message to a contact who is offline is practically the same process as sending a message to a contact that is online.

Not only can you send messages to people when they are not online, other people can send you messages when you're not online. Offline messages are sent in one of two ways. The simplest way is to send the message to the ICQ server. Messages you send will be held there until the intended recipient logs back into the ICQ server. In the same way, messages sent to you while you were offline will be sent to you when you log in.

The other way to send ICQ messages to an offline contact is to send your message as an e-mail message. To do this, your recipient must have his e-mail address in his contact information. The advantage to sending an e-mail message is that most people always at least check their e-mail. Not everyone will load ICQ each time they log in to the Internet. Also, some people abandon an ICQ number and get a new one. Messages sent to abandoned ICQ numbers will wait in an endless queue and for all intents are lost.

I'm a little short of time. Can I send the same message to several people simultaneously?

Sending the same letter to all of your friends rarely fools them, especially when you leave the name blank and write it in using the wrong color ink. But, with ICQ, you can get away with this time-saving act of love without anyone knowing that you've sent the same message to everyone on your list.

Many reasons exist for why you might want to send the same message to some or all of your contacts. Using ICQ as a business tool is a way to keep salespeople up to date on inventory changes or notify customers of special sales. For personal use, ICQ is an excellent way to invite people to parties. Remember that they can even get a map to your house if you've entered your address in your personal user information.

So, save time (and your fingers) by not typing the same message over and over. Sending messages to multiple contacts is pretty simple. Follow these steps:

1. Choose anyone in your **Contact List** by clicking the nickname and selecting **Message** from the popup menu.

2. Write the message you want delivered to multiple people.

3. In the lower-left corner of the message window, click the **More** button, and the message window will expand.

4. Click the button labeled **Multiple Recipients,** located in the lower-right portion of the window (see **Figure 2.2**). Again, the window will expand, but this time to the right. In this new expanded section of the message window will be a list of your contacts, with a check box to the left of their names. Notice that the check box next to the contact you initially chose is already checked.

5. Check each contact you would like to receive this message.

6. Click the **Send** button when you are ready to send the message.

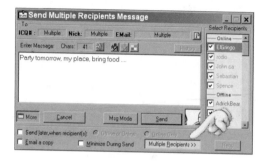

Figure 2.2 Send your message to several people on your Contact List.

ICQ birthday reminders

You will never forget another birthday with this feature. You can customize ICQ to remind you when it is your friend's birthday. You choose when you'd like to be reminded—a few hours before or a few days before the birth date. There's no reason this has to be one-sided. You can also remind your friends when it's your birthday. As long as your ICQ program is running, the ICQ program will remind you even if you are offline. To receive a reminder about your contact's birthday, take these steps:

1. From your **Contact List,** click your contact's nickname to bring up the menu.

2. Click the **User's Details** menu item.

3. From the User Details window, click the tab labeled **More.**

4. If you can see your contact's birthday and horoscope sign, you can check the box option **Remind me (Figure 2.3).** You can choose when you want to be reminded, from 0 day (the same day) to nine days before your contact's birthday. By checking the box, this feature will be all set up.

Figure 2.3
Surprise your friends by remembering their birthdays.

The only thing more fun than remembering your friends' birthdays is having them remember yours. Entering your birthday in your user information enables others to remember your birthday as well. To remind people in your Contact List about your birthday:

1. Click the **ICQ button** in your ICQ window.

2. Click **View/Change My Details.**

3. In the My Details window, select the **More** tab.

4. If you have not entered your birthday, you can do it now. Sorry, but to remind others of your birthday, you have to give up the secret of your age. Of course, you can always fudge the year.

5. After you enter your birth date, the check box beneath the birth date becomes available. Check the **Notify everyone on the day of my birthday** check box.

A message will be sent to everyone in your Contact List on the day of your birthday. If others in your Contact List were also this considerate, you will automatically receive reminders on their birthdays as well.

When the birthday reminder pops onto your screen (see **Figure 2.4**), a whole array of birthday greeting options are available to you:

▶ **Send Message**—The simplest, but still touching, birthday greeting is the traditional ICQ message. Selecting this option will open the message window, in which you can write a personal message to your friend.

▶ **Send Greeting Card**—Using the ICQ Greeting Card plug-in, you can create a birthday card in seconds, complete with a personalized message.

▶ **Visit the ICQ Birthday Center**—This option opens your Web browser and takes you to the ICQ Birthday Center, where you are presented with a wide array of options. In the ICQ Birthday Center page, you can send greeting cards or a free virtual flower bouquet. While you're in the spirit, you can send happy birthday greetings to other members on the ICQ network. If no one remembered your birthday because you forgot to put it in your ICQ user information, you can let others know it's your birthday. There are also links to horoscopes, message boards, recipes, and other cool stuff. Be sure to visit this page when you get a chance.

▶ **Close & Dismiss**—Perhaps you have already thrown the office birthday party, or finished planning a surprise party at home. This event closes the birthday reminder, and it won't appear again until next year.

▶ **Remind Again in**—Perhaps you're busy at the moment and want to be reminded just before you leave the office, so that you can stop and pick up a gift. This option will send you another birthday reminder any time from one minute to seven days. You can choose this option as many times as you like.

Figure 2.4 The birthday reminder can save you from embarrassment.

 Some of my friends are bad about starting their ICQ. Can I also send my message in e-mail to make sure they get it?

Your friends might be on the road and not realize that they can install ICQ on their palm PC so that they can stay in touch with friends and associates all the time. When some of your contacts haven't appeared online for some period of time, it's difficult to know why. It's possible that they changed ICQ numbers and forgot to let you know. It doesn't hurt to send them e-mail to see why they haven't been online or responded to the offline message you sent a few days ago. Rather than look up a contact's e-mail address and then enter it in your e-mail client, ICQ makes sending messages to your contact's e-mail more streamlined (see **Figure 2.5**).

Figure 2.5 Send an ICQ message through e-mail.

Sending an e-mail message delivered through ICQ is very similar to sending a normal ICQ message. Select your contact and write the message as usual. After you write the message, but before you click Send, click the **More** button in the **Send Online Message** window. From the options displayed along the bottom of the message, shown in **Figure 2.5**, check the box labeled **Email a copy.** Then, click **Send,** and your message will be on its way.

Occasionally, an ICQ user will choose to not enter an e-mail address in the ICQ user information. When this happens, you will see that the e-mail address in your ICQ message window is not displayed. If you happen not to notice this and attempt to send your message using e-mail, you will receive the warning shown in **Figure 2.6**.

Figure 2.6 When no e-mail address is available, you will receive this warning.

When you receive a warning that no e-mail address has been specified, you can still enter the user's e-mail address manually in the ICQ e-mail client and continue sending your message through e-mail.

I want to go back and review what someone wrote in a previous message. Can I still see previous messages?

It is often important to go back and review either what people sent in past messages or what you have written to them. Quite often, you'll find yourself reviewing past messages to look for telephone numbers and addresses people have sent you. They could also have given you more detailed information about themselves that was not saved on the ICQ server. There are three ways to review previously sent messages or view your history.

Message Archive

The first way to access your messages is the Message Archive, which keeps a record of every event that has occurred using ICQ. The **Message Archive dialog box** is divided in two or sometimes three windows, depending on the options you use. The first division of the dialog box is the main menu window, located on the left side of the Message Archive, as shown in **Figure 2.7**. The second (top-right) window is the list of events, which displays a list of any events that have occurred for contacts selected from the main menu. This list also displays information such as from whom an event has come or to whom you've sent the event, a brief description, and the date the event occurred. The third (bottom-right) window is where detailed information is displayed about the event selected in the second window. For certain types of information, detailed information is not displayed. In these cases, the third window will not appear, leaving only the main menu and list of events windows.

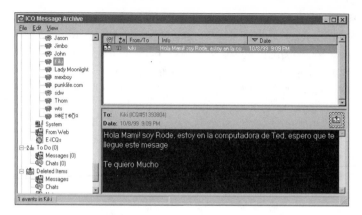

Figure 2.7 The Message Archive is a powerful way to manage past events.

The Message Archive has a list of your contacts. You can access the Message Archive by doing either of the following:

▶ Click the **MyICQ** button in the ICQ window. Select the Message Archive option from the menu.

▶ Click **Open Message Archive.**

▶ Click one of your contacts to bring up the menu. Choose the **History** option and then select **Open Message Archive.**

NOTE

ICQ 2000a implements the Message Archive as a Plug-In. You must download and install the Message Archive before viewing your message history. This plug-in can be downloaded from the ICQ Web site.

The types of events listed in the left window of the Message Archive can be a little confusing. Each type of event is explained in the following sections.

Messages

The first type of event listed in the Message Archive is Messages. Expanding the Messages heading reveals several subheadings, such as MessageDialog, Received, Sent Items, and Sent & Received. Clicking a contact nickname or ICQ number displays events in the top-right window. What might confuse you is that the events listed in this window include more than just messages. The list includes all events, including chats, file transfers, URLs, voice messages, system messages, and ICQ messages. **Table 2.1** describes the different ways to view your events in the Message Archive.

Table 2.1—Options for Viewing the Message Archive

Option Name	Description
Message Dialog	Displays the entire list of messages you have received and sent through ICQ. You'll know who sent the event and at what time. A very handy feature is the information displayed about your response. This list is displayed in chronological order.
Received	Displays only events that you've received, including from whom and when. Different icons let you know what type of event is displayed.
Sent Items	Displays messages and events you have sent, including to whom they were sent and when. Tells you what kind of event you sent by displaying the correct icon.
Sent & Received	Displays all the messages and events you have sent and received. Tells you what kinds of events you have received and sent, including from/to whom and when.

Option Name	Description
System	Displays the system messages you have received or sent. Tells you when you received or sent system messages, the type of system message, and to whom or from whom the message was sent.
From the Web	Displays all the messages, pager messages, or chat requests you have received from the Web. (Either from your Communicator Center Web page or Panel Control, if it is installed on your Web Page.)
E-ICQs	Displays information about to whom or from whom you received an E-ICQ and the date.

2do To Do

The second option in the left window of the Message Archive is 2do ToDo. By marking some message or chats as 2do To Do, ICQ will keep track of the thing you need to do. Usually, you mark messages or chats as **2do ToDo** when, in the message or chat, you discuss things that you need to get done, such as sending flowers to your sister because she just had a baby or calling someone at 9 P.M. to confirm an important business meeting. While you're viewing messages in the Message Archive, you can mark them as 2do ToDo by right-clicking the message and selecting 2do ToDo from the menu. You can also remove items by using the same method and selecting **2do UnMark ToDo** from the menu. Each event that you mark as 2do To Do appears in the 2do ToDo section of the Message Archive for your review. The 2do icon will also appear in the Windows tray along the bottom of the screen, allowing you to open the ICQ 2do list conveniently.

Deleted Items

Deleted Items keeps track of all the items you have deleted. By expanding Deleted Items, you are given three more list options: **Messages, Chats,** and **Notes.** The Messages section contains most of the deleted events, including messages, chat requests, and file requests. The other two options under Deleted Items contain chats and notes that you've deleted.

Notes

Notes contains any notes you've taken using the ICQ Notes feature. In much the same way as you use the 2do feature, you can add almost any event into a note to keep track of it. The text of messages is transferred into a yellow note that resembles a yellow PostIt™ note.

Outbox

Outbox is where all the messages, chats, and other events that are waiting to be sent are kept. If all of your events have been sent, the Outbox appears empty when you click this option. This is an important place to manage events that might be "stuck." You may have messages waiting for months that have not been sent. You can choose to delete them or find another way to deliver them.

Reminder

Reminder is where reminders created using the ICQ Reminder feature are stored. This includes reminders that you have created for yourself and reminders that others have sent you.

Chats

Your saved chats can be accessed by clicking the Chats option, which displays a description of the chat, the participants, and the date the chat took place.

Address Book

The last option is Address Book, which is a list of all of your contacts. This is an efficient way to view contact information. By clicking the contact, you can view the contact's user information. By clicking the Address Book option, you can import and export your address book.

The menu window or first window

Right-clicking any of the options under Messages (Message Dialog, Received, Sent Items, Sent & Received, System, From Web, and E-ICQs) opens a menu with the following selections:

▶ **Open**—Opens or expands that option so that you can see your contacts.

▶ **Open All Items**—Opens all the options. Under every option, you will see your contacts.

▶ **Close All Items**—Closes the options, and you see only the names of the options.

▶ **Advance Find**—Lets you search in all the Message Archives for events.

▶ **A/Z**—Changes the direction of the messages in alphabetical order, received or sent. This option is only valid for Message Dialog.

▶ **Delete All Items**—Sends all the content in that option to the Deleted Items folder. This option works only for System and From Web.

▶ **New Folder**—Creates a new folder in which you can save everything you want. You can give it a name or rename it later on. This option is only valid on the Messages and E-ICQs options.

Section 2 Communicating

Right-clicking 2do To Do opens a menu. The following choices relate to ToDo items:

▶ **Add Personal To Do Event**—Opens a new window in which you can write a new To Do item. Only in the main option.

▶ **Close**—Hides the list of ToDo events in the Message Archive window.

▶ **Unmark All To Do Items**—Erases all the To Do items.

Right-clicking Deleted Items or any of its additional options, such as Messages, Chats, or Notes opens a menu with the following selections:

▶ **Close or Open**—Closes or opens the additional options.

▶ **Empty**—Erases all ICQ events permanently from your computer.

Right-clicking Notes opens a menu with the following selections:

▶ **New Note**—Opens a window in which you can create a new note for yourself.

▶ **Show All**—Opens all the notes.

▶ **Hide All**—Closes all the notes.

▶ **View By Icons**—Displays all the notes from left to right, with an icon and the first words of the notes.

▶ **View By Small Icons**—Same as the previous option, except that it has smaller icons.

▶ **View by list**—The notes have a small icon, but they are in a list form, top to bottom.

▶ **Advanced Find**—Opens a dialog that allows you to search for a specific event in the Message Archive.

Right-clicking Outbox opens a menu with options that will allow you to delete events from the Message Archive:

▶ **Delete All Items**—Sends all the items in this folder to the Deleted Items folder.

▶ **Send Messages Now**—If you are online, you will be able to send the messages that are in your outbox queued to be sent. Occasionally, messages are not sent because your contact is not online and you've chosen the option to send it later.

Right-clicking Reminder opens a menu with the following related choice:

▶ **Add a new reminder**—Opens a window in which you can write a new reminder. Remember that reminders are like ToDo events that will pop up at a specified time and date.

Right-clicking Chats opens a menu with the following related choice:

▶ **Import Chat File**—Opens a window in which you can browse your computer to find and import a chat file into this folder.

Right-clicking Address Book or a contact's name opens a menu with the following choices:

▶ **Import Address Book**—Opens a window in which you can browse to find an Address Book that you had previously saved.

▶ **Export Address Book**—Saves your current Address Book.

▶ **Send E-mail**—Writes and sends e-mail to this contact.

▶ **Rename**—Allows you to change the nickname that appears for your contact.

▶ **Delete**—Erases your contact from the Address Book.

Section 2   Communicating

History from the Contact Window

You can review what was written in previous messages by clicking a particular contact for whom you want to review a message. When you select History from the menu, the following options appear:

▶ **View Messages History**—Opens a new History Events Of <your contact> dialog with three tabs. The Message Dialog tab shows all the messages, both sent and received for that contact, in dialog box form. This is the easiest way to follow conversations you might have had over an extended period of time, without opening each message individually. If you are looking for something particular, you can do a search in this window by clicking the Find button. The date and time of the message are displayed in the first two columns. To remove or display date and time information, click the small calendar icon. In the Incoming and Outgoing tabs, you can view either all incoming or all outgoing events, respectively. These are not limited to only message events.

▶ **Open Message Archive**—Opens the Message Archive, discussed in detail earlier in this section.

▶ **Advance Find**—A much more powerful search than the Search utility in the Message History window. You can select from whom or to whom an event or message was sent. You can search by type of event, such as messages, URLs, chats, files, contacts, external, wwwpager, or Email Express. It's also possible to limit your search to a particular time period or folder, such as Received, Sent Items, Sent & Received, From Web, or Deleted Items.

You can also list the files and URLs a contact has sent to you. Click the option Incoming Files or Incoming Bookmarks. If the contact has not sent you either of these, the menu options will not be available to you.

View History in the message window

A very useful feature is the ability to view message history right from the message window (**Figure 2.8**). Often, as you are typing, you will need to refer to a past message. Click the History button in the upper-right corner of your message window. Your message window will expand, enabling you to view your message history. Also, three new icons will appear to the left of the History button. The calendar icon turns on and off the display of the date and time of the message. The other two icons allow you to advance to the next message or move back to the previous message.

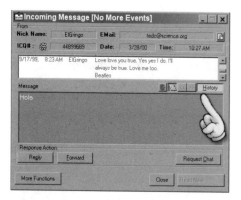

Figure 2.8 View your message history directly in your message window.

Now that I know that my messages stick around, there's personal stuff in there. Can I erase old messages?

Keeping your messages private can be very important, especially when you access the Internet from places such as cyber cafés or work computers. Messages do stick around in the Message Archive, also known as the History. From there, you can view messages, find past messages by using keywords, and save and delete messages. With ICQ, you can erase not only your messages, but all the events, too. You might consider saving the messages to a text file before erasing them. The messages may contain valuable information that you'll want to refer to later. You can erase individual messages, or everything in the Message Archive. A few ways exist to erase messages and other events. Whichever way you choose to erase messages, it's a two-step process. Messages you delete are not deleted immediately. The messages are moved to a Deleted Items folder and held there until you choose to empty the messages in the Deleted Items folder. This is a safeguard against accidentally removing messages you really wanted to keep. But, if you forget about it, you can end up leaving private information on public computers.

Deleting messages from the Message History

To begin, click the nickname in your **Contact List** of the person whose messages you want deleted. Select **History** from the popup menu and then select either **View Messages History** or **Open Message Archive.** Selecting View Messages History shows you only the messages, whereas selecting Open Message Archive displays all types of events, such as file transfers and chat requests.

If you've chosen to View Messages History, a new dialog box appears displaying the messages you've sent to and received from the other party. The new window has three tabs: the MessageDialog tab allows you to view both sent and received messages together, and the other two tabs limit what you see to only incoming or outgoing messages.

To find a particular message, click the **Find** button and enter a keyword or phrase that you believe is in the message you want to delete. This feature will find the first message containing the word or phrase. Each time you click the Find button, you advance to the next message containing your search word or phrase.

After you find the particular message you want to delete, click the message, and the **Delete** button will become available (no longer gray). Click the Delete button. You are asked whether you want to permanently delete the selected message. Clicking the **Yes** button removes the message from the archive; clicking **No** cancels the whole process. Of course, if you saved the Message Archive first, you'll still have another copy of this message.

While viewing the Message History, the **Delete All** button is always active and ready to use. This is a great option to have available for public computers in cyber cafés. If you want every single one of your messages, both incoming and outgoing, erased instantly, click the Delete All button. You will be asked whether this is what you really want to do. Clicking **Yes** erases all the messages in the archive.

CAUTION

We've found a quirk here. Sometimes, when you erase the messages in the Message Archive using the Message History, and then open the Message Archive by selecting Open Message Archive, instead of View Messages History, the messages you thought you had erased are still there to be viewed. Make sure you double check.

Deleting messages from the Message Archive

Using the Message Archive is the most direct way to delete a single message. Open the Message Archive either by clicking the nickname in your Contact List and selecting **History > Open Message Archive,** or by clicking the ICQ button and selecting **History > Message Archive.** In some ways, using the Message Archive can be safer than using the Message History to delete messages. When you click individual messages, you can click the Delete button and, after confirming that you want the message deleted, it will be moved to the Deleted Items folder. You can't select multiple messages and then click Delete. The menu item appears available, but clicking Delete with more than one event or message highlighted does nothing.

To remove all messages and events from a particular contact, you must click the nickname or ICQ number in the list on the left (refer to **Figure 2.9**) with your right-mouse button. Select Delete from the menu, and all the events will be moved to the Deleted Items folder. This removes all events, not just messages. For more information on using the Message Archive, refer to **Question 25**.

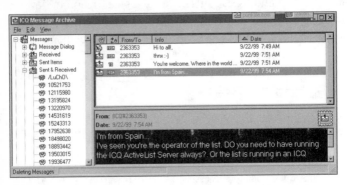

Figure 2.9 In the Message Archive, you can delete all types of events.

Emptying the Deleted Items folder

Emptying the Deleted Items folder is the only way to permanently remove messages and events from your computer. Scroll in the list on the left of the Message Archive window until you see the Deleted Items folder. Click the type of event, such as Messages, beneath Deleted Items. If your Deleted Items list has a plus sign to the left, clicking the plus sign expands the list, to show a list of the different events.

Clicking the type of event displays a list of the events in the window on the right. You now have several choices:

▶ Restore the event by right-clicking the event and selecting Restore from Deleted from the menu.

▶ Remove a single item permanently by right-clicking and selecting Delete from the menu.

▶ Move the item to another folder by right-clicking and selecting Move to or Copy to from the menu.

You can do many other things with the events in the list. Simply right-click and select from the menu. If you want to remove all the items in your Deleted Items folder, right-click the type of event in the list beneath Deleted Items and select Empty from the menu. After confirming that you really want to get rid of these messages, they will be permanently removed—for real this time.

Chatting

Until everyone in the world has a super-fast Internet connection, chatting will remain one of the Internet's favorite pastimes. From the earliest days of home computers, people have found a way to chat, first through bulletin board software, then through the Internet's IRC (Internet Relay Chat), and now through powerful chat programs like the one included in ICQ.

 **I've heard of chat rooms. Do I have to go in a chat room to chat with my friends?**

One of the nicest things ICQ does for you is keep you out of crowded and smoky chat rooms. You can have your own private chat with the ICQ program. Chat only with the people you contact. No longer do you have to try to fit your chat into a public chat room filled with other people talking nonsense.

Requesting a chat

First, select from your **Contact List** the person whom you'd like to chat with by clicking the nickname to bring up the menu. Click **ICQ chat,** and the **Send Online Chat Request** window appears, in which you explain your reason for requesting the chat in the **Enter Chat Subject** area (see **Figure 2.10**). When you're ready to request the chat, click the **Chat** button. A little window (called the ICQ Chat Module) with the ICQ faces icon appears while contacting, asking for permission, and getting the chat information from your contact.

When your chat request has been accepted, an informational dialog box appears letting you know that chat information is being exchanged. Once the session has been established, the chat window will appear. You can now start chatting. If the other side does not accept your chat request, a message window will appear telling you that the user has declined your request to chat. Try not to feel bad.

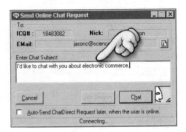

Figure 2.10 Tell your contact what you'd like to talk about.

Receiving a chat request

When you get a chat request, ICQ first announces the request with the "Incoming chat request" sound. The incoming chat request message displays the nickname, e-mail address, and ICQ number of the person requesting the chat with you. Sometimes your contact will give a reason for chatting, but this is not required.

If you don't feel like chatting, you can choose to not accept the chat. The incoming chat request window gives you several options for refusing the chat. Clicking the Do Not Accept button will present you with options for letting the other party know you aren't feeling chatty.

Depending on your attitude toward the person you are refusing to chat with, you can choose from the following messages that will be displayed on the other person's computer:

▶ **Decline without giving a reason**—This is a flat rejection. "Go away, I don't want to chat with you."

▶ **Decline, giving a reason**—"Sorry, but I'm doing my nails, washing my hair, try again later."

▶ **Reply with an away message**—This is like letting the answering machine answer your phone. "No, I don't want to talk, and I don't feel like coming up with an excuse."

▶ **Entering your own reason to decline**—This is the most humane way of letting someone down. This is where you get to pour your heart out. "My dog is on the way to the hospital and I must chase the ambulance on the way to the veterinary hospital. I'd love to stay and chat with you, but, you understand..."

Of course, you can always just chat. If you decide to chat, click Accept, and the ICQ Chat Module will appear. The module will make the connection with your contact so that you can start chatting.

The first time that you use ICQ chat, it appears in **Internet Relay Chat (IRC)** mode (see **Figure 2.11**). IRC is one of the original ways for people to chat over the Internet. Early in the history of the Internet, IRC was a powerful and complicated chat interface. Volumes have been written about IRC. Many of the modern chat utilities, such as ICQ, have features that were modeled after IRC. The programmers at ICQ make no bones about the fact that they have patterned their chat after IRC. You can switch between chat styles: modern-simple or old-style IRC. Each chat message in IRC mode is preceded by the nickname of the person chatting. In IRC mode, you type your text in the window along the bottom, and each time you hit the Enter key, your text is sent and appears in the side-by-side panes above the bottom pane.

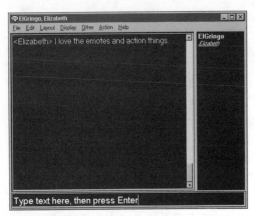

Figure 2.11 Chat window in IRC mode.

While IRC chat is an excellent interface for chatting with large groups of people, when you want to converse with one person, we recommend using one of the other chat styles, such as Split, Vertical, or Horizontal mode. These other styles are easier to read and follow. In these other modes, you and your chat partner each have your own chat windows in which you can type continuously and simultaneously.

There are two ways to change chat modes. After you launch your chat session, your chat window may or may not be displaying a toolbar of useful icons. This toolbar is very useful while chatting and has features not available from the menus. If twelve small icons do not appear across the top of your chat window, we recommend turning them on now, by choosing **Layout > Toolbar.**

If you can see the toolbar, click the **Style** icon, represented by a square divided in two with a blue color on the top half of the square and black on the bottom half. Clicking this icon opens the **IRC/Split Style** window (see **Figure 2.12**), which tells you the current style you are in and lets you change to the other style.

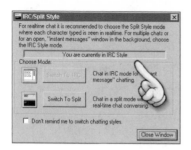

Figure 2.12 Click the mode button associated with the style of chat you would like.

You can also change the chat style from the menu on the chat window. Click **Layout,** and a list of options will appear. Choose the style of your chat by clicking the name of the style.

Traditional chat rooms

If you prefer to chat with a group of people in a traditional chat room, ICQ offers that, too. There are chat rooms created by ICQ members. Add them to your list, and every time they are online, you can participate in their chats. You can find the chat rooms sorted by interest at **www.icq.com/icqchat/**.

Don't be shy—set up your own IrCQ chat room where anyone can join in. You can meet many fun people. IrCQ chat has been built right into the World Wide Web. When you create your own IrCQ chat room, the address is the same as your ICQ homepage. Anyone visiting your ICQ homepage can join the chat. We tell you how to set up your ICQ homepage later in the book.

Making chat friends

Another cool chat feature in ICQ is random chat. While writing this book, we made some nice friends all over the world using the random chat feature. When people configure their ICQ to accept random chat, they are letting people on the ICQ network know that they are ready to chat and make friends with strangers. You can choose from many different chat topics to find someone interested in the same things you are. These chats are mostly one-on-one, but occasionally people invite everyone to join in the chat.

To find a Chat with a Friend:

1. Click the **Online** status button to launch the status menu.

2. From the top of the status menu select **Chat with a Friend.**

3. Select **Find a Chat Partner.** This launches the Chat with a Friend window.

4. Select the **Details** tab and select a group of people to search in, and optionally enter a chat topic.

5. Edit your personal information as it appears in this window. This is the information that will be available to people who accept your chat invitation.

6. Select the **Finding** tab and click the **Find an Online Chat Friend** button to begin your search.

7. After ICQ finds someone, you can view some of the details they may have entered about themselves (**Figure 2.13**). If this person does not sound like someone you'd like to chat with, you can search again. As soon as you select someone you would like to chat with, select one of the following:

   —**Request a Chat**—Chat with a Friend still get to decide whether they want to chat with you. Don't get discouraged if you're turned down a few times. Some people are already chatting and don't need a second chat partner.

   —**Send Message**—You might precede your chat attempt with a message introducing yourself and setting up a time later to chat.

   —**Send URL**—This is a good way to send someone your ICQ homepage and invite them to join your IrCQ Web chat.

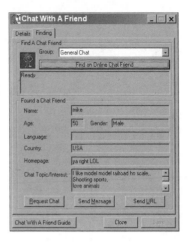

Figure 2.13 View information about new chat partners in the Chat with a friend window.

 **Can I chat with more than one person at a time?**

One of the really nice things about ICQ's chat is the capability to easily have a private chat between two people, have a chat among a private group of people, or join into a public chat room that is discussing topics that interest you. You first have to be chatting with someone, before you can invite others to join your chat. This means that a chat must be running before a third or fourth person can join in. Then, you have three ways to let additional people join the chat:

▶ If you are chatting with someone and you want another friend from your Contact List to join in, send a chat request as you normally would, but click the Join Session button rather than the Chat button in the chat request window.

▶ While chatting with someone, if another person sends you a chat request, you can choose to have the new requester join your existing chat. Accept the chat request by clicking the Add to Session button rather than the Accept button in the chat request window.

▶ For either of the preceding options, you can choose which chat session you want your contact to join by selecting from the drop-down menu shown in **Figure 2.14**. This menu lists all of your chat sessions by the names of the participants.

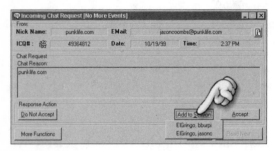

Figure 2.14 Choose the chat session in which you want your contact to participate.

▶ You can drag the nickname from your Contact List to the chat window—but be warned that this option does not always work. If this fails, you can fall back on one of the two previous methods of adding chat partners.

You should be able to see the nicknames of all of your chat partners. If you are in IRC mode, all the names will be listed along the right side of your chat window. If you are using any of the Split modes, you see a window for each contact, as shown in **Figure 2.15**.

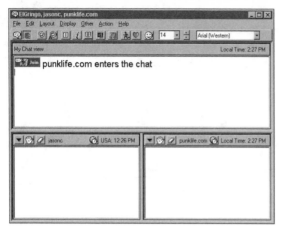

Figure 2.15 Three-way chat in Split mode.

I am having trouble reading the small fonts. How can I make the text look different?

You don't have to break out the reading glasses to read small text scrolling through your chat window. Also, you can change the color of the font and the background color so that it will be easier to read. There are two ways to change the font size and the style of the font.

The first and easiest way is if you have the toolbar displayed. You will see the size and style of the font in the top-right corner of the chat window. By clicking the drop-down arrow next to the font name, the list of fonts that you have installed on your computer will appear in the drop-down list. Select the font name from the list. You may also choose the size you want the text to appear by selecting it from the list of font sizes, again using the drop-down menu. You may notice that not all font sizes are available for every font. Some fonts are limited to specific font sizes or even a single font size.

If you don't have the toolbar displayed, select **Display from the chat window** menu. Choosing fonts from the drop-down menu will launch the font selection window. Select the font style and size and click OK when you have finished.

> **TIP**
>
> To turn on the toolbar, click Layout from the chat window menu. Click again on Toolbar so that a check mark appears to the left of the menu selection. You might have to click the menu again to see the check mark.

If you're the type of person who likes to make a point by underlining or bolding your text to add meaning and expression, you can decorate your text by bolding, underlining, and italicizing in ICQ. Change your text decoration either by clicking the toolbar icons or by selecting your text. Using the toolbar to change the color of the fonts and background is simple. To change the background color, simply click the palette icon, which reveals a menu of sixteen possible colors for you to choose from. To change your font color, click the palette icon, which has the letter *A* in the bottom-left corner. Select from the list of colors. Not all text colors can be seen well on some of the brighter or darker background colors. Experiment until you find the right combination.

 **My aesthetic sense has been violated by the colors my friends use when chatting. Can I override their bad taste?**

Everyone has a different sense of what looks good and what does not. Sometimes, we use a font that we think is incredible but others think is ugly or very difficult to read. Some people use vibrant text and background colors that, after a while, can bother your eyes. The good thing is that font color and background selection are a matter of personal taste that can be overridden. You neither have to change your font and color choices when someone complains, nor put up with someone's attempt to be artistic.

To override another person's text font style and color-combination preferences, click the small icon that is second from the left (it looks like Zorro meets air conditioning duct) in your chat window toolbar. You can also select **Display > Override Format** from the chat menu (see **Figure 2.16**).

Figure 2.16 Two ways to override another person's chat preferences.

How do people make all of those funny noises while they're chatting with me?

It isn't actually people making the noises, it's the computer. If your friends have short attention spans, and their favorite TV show captures their interest while chatting, grab their attention by blasting them with a car horn. At the top of the chat window, select from the Other menu. From this menu, you can beep the user on the other end with an "ahhooga" sound. You can also beep the other user by pressing the Ctrl key and G key together **(Ctrl+G)**.

When something strikes you as funny, the person on the other end of the chat can't actually hear you laughing, but you can send the next best thing. Select LOL (laugh out loud) from the **Other** menu, or hit **Ctrl+L.**

Chatting seems so dry and unemotional. Is there a way to add emotion?

Early electronic chatters developed a shorthand to cut down on the number of key strokes it would take to express an emotion. Abbreviations such as ttyl (talk to you later), brb (be right back), LOL (laugh out loud), and others have filled chats for years.

ICQ has made this shorthand easy. You no longer have to learn the cryptic abbreviations. You can send actions and emotions with a simple menu click. Send an action quickly by using the key combination **Ctrl+A.** Select an action from the list, and a message will appear in the chat. The message appears next to the action graphic.

Clicking the heart icon in your chat window lets you include some fun gestures. These appear like actions in the chat but include a sound that is played for your chat partner. Including gestures is fun and adding multimedia to your chat makes the chat more personal. Choose to be annoyed, disgusted or one of many other emotions. Mix and match gestures with emoticons.

The *emoticon*, another type of abbreviation that was born in the world of Internet chat, is a picture drawn with letters and characters. The most famous of the emoticons is the smiley face :-). This has become so common that the smiley face is seen everywhere: in advertisements, letters, and, of course, in chat sessions. Other emoticons such as the wink ;-) and the sad face :-(are also very common. (See **Figure 2.17.**)

smile
laughing
frown
angry
very angry
my lips are sealed
wink
kiss
nosy
wearing shades
shocked
sticking out tongue
confused
piggy

Figure 2.17 Have fun with smileys.

Creating complex emoticons has been a favorite pastime for many on the Internet. You're still welcome to participate in this pastime. For those who simply want to express their feelings, ICQ has added the ability to insert smiley faces. To insert a smiley face, you must first make certain that your toolbar is showing in your chat window. Then click the bright yellow happy face button and select the smiley that fits your mood.

 **We talked about interesting things in this chat. Is there a way to save it?**

Saving your chat sessions so you can refer back to them later is one of the abilities you have with ICQ chat. Not only can you read entire text versions of the chat, you can also watch the entire chat session replay itself just as it did originally.

At the end of your chat, you are given an opportunity to name and save your chat session. This is done differently depending on who closes the chat. If you close the chat, you have two choices: close without saving and close, saving the chat. If you choose to save, you're asked to name the chat. You can give it a long, meaningful name, such as "my chat with Louie about finances." You are not asked where to save the chat, because it saved within ICQ, not as a file.

Section 2 Communicating

Voices

Not everyone likes to type or read text on the screen. We have become accustomed to speaking with our friends and associates on the telephone, and the idea of typing messages can feel impersonal and labor-intensive. Even though text isn't dead yet, ICQ includes the very powerful ability to send and receive voice messages. Sending and receiving voice messages isn't as efficient as chatting or sending messages, but it has its advantages when it comes to hearing emotions, sounds, or the gurgle of a newborn baby.

 **I type about two words an hour. Can I just send someone a voice message?**

Yes, there is an ICQ option called **Voice Message** that allows you to send spoken messages rather than written ones. There are no limits on how many voice messages you can send or on the size of your message. You can say a few words or quote entire Shakespearean monologues. There are two things you should take into consideration when sending a voice message. The first consideration is that both you and your contact must be online. You can't send a voice message to a contact who is offline—this is an online feature only.

Second, depending on the length of your voice message, the time it takes to send the message and for your contact to download can be considerable. Voice messages tend to require a large number of bytes, making the transfer time something you should be aware of.

To send a voice message:

1. Click the contact to whom you'd like to send a voice message.

2. From the menu, click **Voice Message** (remember, your contact has to be online to use this feature), and the Voice Message window will launch.

3. From the Voice Message window, you can either record a voice message or send a prerecorded WAV file. By default, you must record a new voice message.

4. Click the **Record** button and start talking into your microphone. The Record button is the small square button with the red circle on it, as shown in **Figure 2.18**.

5. When you have finished recording your message, click the **Stop** button (with the small square icon, positioned next to the Record button).

6. You have the option of including text along with your voice message. Hardcore chat people can't resist a place to type a message.

7. Click **Send,** and your message will be on its way.

You can play your voice message back before sending, to make sure you sound good. You can play the whole voice message or part of it. Also, you can check on how big the voice message is so that you can give yourself an idea of how long it's going to take for your contact to download it.

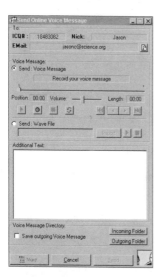

Figure 2.18 ICQ Send Online Voice Message window, ready to record and send your message.

To send a WAV file:

1. Follow the first two steps for sending a voice message.

2. Click the radio button **Send: Wave File.**

3. Click the **Import** button.

4. Choose the WAV file you want to send from the file dialog box that appears when you clicked the Import button. Note that WAV files generally have a .wav file extension (the last three letters on the end of a filename).

5. Preview the WAV file by clicking the **Play** button.

6. In the space below, you can type some information about the file or just a few words to your contact.

7. Click **Send,** and you are done.

You can save the outgoing voice message by checking the box labeled **Save outgoing Voice Message** on the bottom of the window.

Q35 What do I need to have to use the voice feature?

The ICQ software supports the voice message. You need the plug-in that comes with newer versions of ICQ and, more importantly, you need the required sound hardware installed in your computer. In case you don't have the plug-in installed in your computer, or if you want to find out which plug-ins you have installed in ICQ, do the following:

1. Click the **ICQ button** on the bottom-left corner of your ICQ window.

2. Select **Preference & Security** from the popup menu.

3. Click **Preferences,** and the Owner Preference window will appear.

4. Select the **Plugins tab.** In this window, you can see which plug-ins you have installed in ICQ. You also can see a description of each plug-in and what it does. You can have some fun by customizing the sound that plays when the plug-in is contacted by an event. Also, you can add more plug-ins or erase the ones you already have. If you want to add a plug-in, keep following these steps.

5. Click the **Add** button and a browse window will open.

6. In the Browse window, navigate to the folder where you installed ICQ (normally located in the Program Files folder). Within the directory where ICQ is installed you will find a folder called **Plugins.** Open this folder.

7. Within the Plugins folder, opened in Step 6, each plug-in will appear in its own folder. Open the folder containing the plug-in you want to install. For example, if you want to install the Voice Message plug-in, open the VoiceMessage folder.

8. Plug-ins are stored in special dynamic link library files (DLLs). The DLL file for Voice Message is named ICQVoice.dll. Open this file. This will start the installation, or *activation,* as ICQ calls it.

9. A caution window will appear, warning you about plug-ins developed by third parties. Read through the caution message and click Yes if you wish to continue. The VoiceMessage DLL can be trusted.

10. If the activation was successful, you are notified that the plug-in was successfully installed. Click the **Close** button. The ICQ plug-in you installed should appear listed in the Owner Preferences window.

Closer Look at the Plugins Tab

Plug-ins are the way ICQ is extended. Getting comfortable with adding plug-ins is important. From the Plugins tab on the Owners Preferences window, you can see the ICQ plug-ins that you have activated. You will see the plug-ins listed down the left side of this tab. Clicking the name of the plug-in displays a brief description.

Sounds are one of the ways ICQ alerts you to an incoming event. Some events are handled by ICQ plug-ins, and you can customize the way you are notified. In the Plugins tab is a check box labeled Play Sound. When this is checked, it will play the sound file indicated by the filename entered in the box next to it. This sound plays each time that an event the selected plug-in is meant to handle arrives on your computer. You can preview the sound by clicking the little black arrow before the filename. To change the sound you want to play, click the little button with three dots after the filename. This opens a window that allows you to browse your computer in search of the sound file you want played.

You may consider creating your own sound files using the Windows Sound Recorder. Record yourself saying something like, "Incoming voice message." You will find the Sound Recorder by selecting **Start > Programs > Accessories > Entertainment > Sound Recorder.** After you create the sound file, enter the path and filename to play this sound each time a plug-in is launched by an event.

You can also tell ICQ what to do when an event handled by a plug-in arrives. Some plug-ins have more configurable options than others. Here are the options for the three most used ICQ plug-ins:

▶ **Greeting Card**—By default, Show Respond Dialog
is selected. Each time you get a Greeting Card, a
Dialog window asks whether you want to accept
this event. There are no other options for this
plug-in.

▶ **ICQmail**—Like the Greeting Card plug-in, by
default, Show Respond Dialog is selected.

▶ **Voice Message**s—This dialog box has additional
configurable options. You can configure the Show
Respond Dialog option as in the other plug-ins.
You can also choose to Auto Accept or Auto
Decline Voice Message events. If you don't want
to be bothered by incoming voice messages from
people who are not in your Contact List, you can
choose Auto Decline For Users Not In My Contact
List. With this option selected, ICQ pays attention
only to voice messages from users in your list.

The Voice Messages plug-in has additional options.
If you click the button labeled More, a Voice Message
preferences window will launch. The version of the
Voice Message plug-in you are using is displayed along
with a brief description. This window has two options.
You can choose to save outgoing voice messages and
incoming voice messages by checking the
corresponding check boxes.

Add or remove ICQ plug-ins by clicking either the Add or
Remove buttons below the list of plug-ins. As a panic
button measure, when all else fails, you can restore all
the ICQ defaults by clicking the very large button at the
bottom of the Preferences window. Be aware that this
button restores defaults for all preferences, not just plug-
ins. Restoring ICQ defaults removes any customization
you have done by setting preferences. It will not affect
either your contacts or your History.

Once you're done, click OK and everything will be saved.

Most newer computers come complete with all the sound hardware you need to be able to use the voice features of ICQ. If for some reason your computer does not have the required hardware, these items are available for very little money at any computer store.

The first thing you must have is a sound card. In **Question 36**, we guide you through the process of discovering whether your computer has a sound card and explain some basic sound card features. If your computer has a sound card, it needs speakers for you to be able to hear any of the sounds coming from your sound card. Because a sound card does not provide any amplification of the sound it produces, the sound card must first be connected to either an amplifier or, more commonly, powered speakers with built-in amplifiers. Amplified speakers come in all sizes and shapes and sometimes even come attached to your monitor. As with most things, your budget will determine the quality of your speakers. Some speaker systems come complete with subwoofers and 3-D surround-sound.

Important to the quality of your voice conversation is the microphone you use. There are many microphones designed specifically for computers. We've written an introduction to microphones in **Question 37**.

Q36   Are all sound cards the same?

Sound cards extend a computer's capability to make noises other than the hum of the fan, the grinding of the hard drives, the rattle of the case, and the ubiquitous 440 hertz beep from the internal speaker. Nearly all computers today come with sound cards installed. If you are curious to know whether your computer has a sound card, it does if it has stereo speakers and can play music or make interesting sounds at startup or shutdown. If you still aren't certain whether your computer has a sound card, take a look at the back of your computer where everything plugs in (see **Figure 2.19**). Before PCs with Pentium processors, sound cards were an add-on that had to be purchased and installed separately.

Game Port

Speaker Output

Microphone Input

Headphone Output

Figure 2.19 Most sound cards look similar when viewed from the back of your computer.

Why do I need a sound card with ICQ?

Sound cards are not absolutely required for use with ICQ, but ICQ will use one if you have it installed. ICQ has a rich supply of sounds and voice messages that let you know when an event has taken place. For example, when a message arrives, you hear the famous ICQ "Uh oh." When someone requests a chat, you will hear a voice saying "Incoming chat request." These sounds and messages are completely configurable, but without a sound card, you will never hear them.

What are the main differences in sound cards?

Sound cards have three main abilities:

▶ **Accept sound input**—This input can be from sound files on your computer; from a microphone; from your computer's CD player, DVD player, or TV card; or from some external sound devices, such as a stereo. Each sound card is a little different, but most of them have a place to plug in a microphone. Often, the sound card has places where your computer's CD player, DVD player, and sometimes even a computer television tuner card can plug in. Your computer most likely came with all of these devices already configured. The only thing you might be required to do is plug in a microphone and speakers. The electronic circuitry on the sound card has the ability to convert the digital information in sound files (such as WAV files), Internet phone, and streaming digital media (such as Real Media files) into analog form before it is sent to your computer's speakers. The sound card also has the ability to accept sound information, already in analog form, such as from microphones and stereos, and send this information out through its output ports to your speakers. The analog information from stereos and microphones can also be digitized using programs like the Windows Sound Recorder.

▶ **Generate their own sounds**—Most sound cards have special circuitry to process Musical Interface Digital Interface (MIDI) commands. MIDI is a special digital command language used by high-tech musical instruments that tells synthesizers what kind of noise to make, including the pitch, duration, volume, and quality, to emulate certain instruments, such as a piano or a drum. Some sound cards have very sophisticated MIDI synthesizers that can play hundreds of sounds, whereas others play the basic sixty-four MIDI sounds.

▶ **Output the sounds they either receive or generate**— Because sound cards don't have amplifiers in them, the sound that is output must be played through either headphones or an amplifier. The sound quality between sound cards does not vary much. The one important difference is something called *duplex*. If a sound card has the ability to send and receive files simultaneously, it is called *full-duplex*. Your telephone is full-duplex, because you can talk while simultaneously listening to the person on the other end talk. (Some conversations with my mother are often much shorter because of the full-duplex capability of telephones.) Older sound cards are *single-duplex*, meaning they have the ability to receive or send, but not both at the same time. Full-duplex capability is important if you want to use the voice chat capability of some ICQ plug-ins. Otherwise, both single- and full-duplex sound cards work fine for ICQ's sound and voice messaging capabilities.

Q37   What kind of microphone should I use?

Most computer microphones are called *condenser* microphones and are inexpensive. The one requirement is that the microphone you choose must have a connection that is compatible with your sound card, and most sound cards accept miniplug connections. Many types and qualities of microphones are available for computers. On the high end are wireless microphones, which leave you completely free to roam about the room while you talk. Combine this fancy microphone with a wireless keyboard and wireless mouse and you have complete mobility.

When using ICQ for voice applications, we have found it very useful to use one of the combination headsets. The combination of headphones and a microphone keeps your conversation private and gives you more freedom of movement around your computer. Most desktop microphones require you to be pretty close when you speak into them. The headset has an attached microphone that is positioned at all times in front of your mouth.

If you want to select a quality microphone, look for the
frequency response of the microphone. The frequency response
is the range of sound from low to high that the microphone is
able to detect. The human ear can hear sounds ranging from
20 hertz to 20,000 hertz. A good condenser microphone has a
range of 50 hertz to 15,000 hertz.

TIP

Some condenser microphones use a battery. If you own a
condenser microphone, check the battery every couple of
months.

Unwanted Guests

In articles we've read about ICQ, mention is made of the fact
that ICQ leaves you open to a new kind of unwanted
communication in the form of spam. It's true that ICQ, being a
powerful and popular communication tool, does open the door
for discourteous people to bother you. Unlike other forms of
Internet communication, such as e-mail, ICQ has a rich set of
tools built in to help you avoid receiving unwanted
communications.

**I'm constantly bothered by strangers
trying to sell me things. Is there a way I
can ignore them?**

There are many enterprising people on the Internet, and not all
of them are courteous. Unfortunately, because of these few
people, we must take steps to ensure the quality of our own
Internet experience. Yes, you can ignore them. In fact, not only
can you ignore them, you can ask ICQ to ignore them so that
you never hear them again. ICQ has a feature called **Ignore List,**
which contains the names, nicknames, and ICQ numbers of

people you decide to ignore. People on your Ignore List can't send you any type of event. There are two ways to put people on the Ignore List, depending on whether or not they are also in your Contact List.

When they are not part of your Contact List

When you receive a message or some other event from someone who is not in your Contact List, they will appear in your Contact List under Not In List. By clicking their name, you can customize your interaction with them in ways that are not available to you for people who you've selected to put in your Contact List. From your Contact List, you can do the following:

▶ Receive the events they send

▶ Add them to your Contact List

▶ Add them to your Address Book

▶ Move them to the Ignore List

▶ Send messages to them

▶ Send them URLs

▶ Send your contacts to them

▶ Send them e-mail

▶ See the History of events with them

▶ See their homepage

▶ See their user details

When you receive a message from someone not in your Contact List, you have different options on the message window. Notice the addition buttons in **Figure 2.20** allowing you to add someone to your Ignore List or add them to your Contact List.

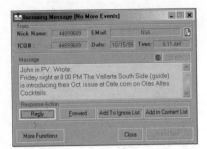

Figure 2.20 Messages from people not in your Contact List have additional options.

Just like exchanging messages with people already in your Contact List, you can view the user information of the person who sent the message to you. Of course, you can reply to the message and even forward the message to someone else in your Contact List. Additionally, you can add this person to your Ignore List, and chances are good that you'll never hear from this particular ICQ number ever again. Of course, nothing stops people from getting a new ICQ number and contacting you again. Persistence pays off, though. Just keep adding unwanted guests to your Ignore List.

Of course, if the message is from someone you'd like to add to your Contact List, you can choose to add them by clicking the Add to Contact List button. If the person automatically accepts requests to be added to your Contact List, ICQ will do it immediately. Otherwise, you'll have to go through the approval process, where the user can elect whether or not to allow you to add them.

You have all the powerful ICQ functions at your fingertips, even with people who are not in your Contact List. You can do any of the following:

▶ Archive this message to the folder you want

▶ Create this message as a note

▶ Add this message to the 2do To Do list

▶ Add this message as a reminder

▶ Print this message

▶ Delete all incoming events

When you need to ignore someone already in your Contact List

Sometimes we decide to add a contact to our list because we believe the person is nice and someone who we'd like to communicate with. But alas, even being the social creatures we are, there are just some people with whom we don't get along. Some of the people we've added have sent us thousands of bad URLs and phony virus warnings, and the worst part is that they won't answer our messages. So, if this contact doesn't want to talk with you and is sending trash every minute, onto the Ignore List they go.

The process of ignoring someone who is already on your Contact List as a normal contact has more steps than does ignoring people who are not on your Contact List. There are two ways to go about this. Here is the fastest way:

1. Click the **ICQ button** menu in the bottom of your ICQ window.

2. Select **Security and Privacy.**

3. In the Security window that appears, click the tab labeled **Ignore List.** This is where all the information about people you want to ignore is saved.

4. This is where it gets a little tricky. With the Security window open and your Contact List open, click and drag to the Ignore List the contact you want to ignore. Then, release the mouse button over the Ignore List.

5. You will receive a confirmation that you are about to add a new person to your Ignore List. Click **Yes** to continue, and ICQ will erase all of the contact's History, remove him from your Contact List, and enter him into your Ignore List.

Section 2 Communicating

The other way to add people to your Ignore List allows you to add them before they ever contact you. It also lets you find and add to your Ignore List all ICQ numbers of a particular ICQ user. Launch the Security and Privacy window by following the first four steps just listed. Then, click the **Add to Ignore List** button from the Ignore List tab.

Clicking the Add to Ignore List button opens a search window in which you are prompted to enter information identifying the contact you want to add to your Ignore List. You can search by e-mail address, nickname, first name, last name, or ICQ number. Depending on the information you enter, you might get a large list of people. Choose carefully from the list, selecting the person you believe is the one you want added to your Ignore List. The most exact method of searching is by ICQ number. Because the ICQ number is unique, it can return only a single result. The e-mail address is most likely to turn up the person you are looking for and all of the associated ICQ numbers. Remember to add them all to your Ignore List. Searching by nickname is a less effective way of finding the person you'd like to ignore, because of the number of duplicate nicknames on the ICQ network. (Sometimes, you have to pay a lot of attention to the person you'd like to ignore.)

The same people I ignored yesterday have a new ICQ number and are bothering me again. Now what?

It can be a pain in the neck getting messages or URLs from people you don't know and, in some cases, don't want to know. You can get tired of people trying to sell you stuff or wanting you to visit their pornographic Web site. There are people who spend a great deal of time and effort sending unwanted ICQ messages. The Internet is often referred to as a place, or as a virtual place: *cyberspace*. Many people spend much of their lives working or playing in cyberspace and consider it part of their home or office.

It's important to be able to control the kinds of people with whom we interact in this extension of our physical world.

Choosing to ignore individuals, as described in the previous question, can take care of certain bothersome users. But these same individuals quite often change ICQ numbers several times a day. ICQ makes it possible to avoid messages from these people in a more global manner.

Launch the **Security and Privacy** window by following these three steps:

1. Click the **ICQ button** menu in the bottom of your ICQ window.

2. Select **Preferences & Security** from the popup menu.

3. Select **Security and Privacy.**

One simple way to avoid getting messages from strangers is to select the option labeled Accept messages only from users in my Contact List. You will continue to receive messages from the people in your Contact List, while messages or other events such as URLs sent by people not in your Contact List will be rejected automatically. You will never even realize that something was sent and rejected. But you still can get requests from people to add them to your Contact List.

These are other options you can check on the Ignore List tab:

▶ **Do not accept Multi-Recipient Messages from either all users or users not in my contact list**—You get a *multirecipient* message when someone sends the same message to multiple people at the same time. When you choose to send the same message to multiple people in your Contact List, you are sending a multirecipient message. Choosing this option is one way to stop getting annoying messages from overzealous friends who like to send constant messages to everyone on their list. If this practice is not obnoxious enough to put them on your Ignore List, you can choose to block all multirecipient messages, or only those sent to you by people not in your Contact List.

▶ **Do not accept WWP messages**—Your World-Wide Pager
will be deactivated and people won't be able to contact you
using this feature from your Web page. You may enjoy many
of the features afforded by having an ICQ-enabled Web page,
but you may want to limit your communications to people
who are registered on the ICQ network.

▶ **Do not accept E-mail Express Messages**—Like the
preceding option, people won't be able to contact you
through your E-Mail Express. We find that E-Mail Express is
very handy for people who do not have ICQ installed and
want to contact us using ICQ. However, if you are
experiencing a great deal of unwanted correspondence
through E-Mail Express, you may choose to turn it off, either
permanently or long enough to discourage the sender.

▶ **Do not allow direct communication with previous (less
secure) client**—In case someone has a less secure or older
version of ICQ, this option won't let them have direct
communications with you. They can send messages through
the server, but they won't be able to chat with you.

Sending Files

With ICQ, you have the ability to send files online to your
contacts. Send as many files as you want. ICQ is able to send
any file, of any size and in any format. You can send pictures,
documents, MP3 files, Zip files, or anything in a computer file
format. The file is sent as a peer-to-peer file transfer, a direct
connection between your computer and your contact's
computer. There is no way to send a file through the ICQ server.

How can I use ICQ to send someone a file?

It's simple and easy to send files through ICQ. You may decide, while chatting, to send a photo or document to the person you're chatting with. File transfers can take place while you use other ICQ features. Because the file transfer takes place peer to peer without involving the ICQ server, the one requirement is that both computers be online and connected to the ICQ network. Follow the next steps to send a file:

1. Click your contact's nickname to bring up the contact menu.

2. From the menu, click the **File** option.

3. Two windows will pop up—the **Send File Request** dialog window and a dialog window titled Open (the file browse window). In the Open dialog, locate and select the file you want to send.

4. After selecting the file, click the **Open** button. This closes the window and inserts the file information into the **Send Online File Request** window, shown in **Figure 2.21**.

Figure 2.21 The online file request will be sent before you can send your file.

In the Send Online File Request window, you can see the ICQ number, the nickname, and the e-mail address of your contact. The user information icon is there for your convenience. You also can view the name and the size of the file you are about to send. In the text box provided, you can enter an optional short description of the file or a short message. Once you're ready to request the file transfer, click Send.

After you click the Send button, a "Waiting for the other side to reply" message appears at the bottom of the window, letting you know that the other side has not yet accepted the file transfer. As soon as your file transfer request is accepted, a new window opens displaying the filename, number of files, and the progress of the file transfer.

When ICQ finishes sending the file, you get a confirmation telling you that the transfer is complete. This confirmation includes the time and date of the transfer, the name of the file or files that were transferred, and the description you entered. Click OK, and the window will close. That's all there is to ICQ file transfer. It's quite painless.

You can send more than one file at a time. However, there is one restriction about sending multiple files: the files you are sending have to be in the same folder on your computer. If the files you want to send are in different folders, you will be unable to select them all. You can send additional file transfers, but it might be easier to move the files into a single folder and avoid multiple file transfers.

There is no file size restriction, but the smaller the file, the faster it transfers. ICQ will tell you approximately how much time it's going to take to send your file and the speed at which it's being sent.

 My connection is pretty slow. Can I do other things while the file is being sent?

There is no restriction to what you can do while your file is transferring. Curl your hair, paint your nails, check your e-mail, send messages, chat, browse the Internet, or use your computer. Using your computer heavily might slow down your ICQ file transfer, however. We recommend that you don't use your connection to the Internet heavily while you are sending a large file (more than 1MB).

The speed of your connection to the Internet and the speed of your contact's connection will determine the speed of the file transfer. For example, you could have a fast connection using a cable modem, but if your contact connects to the Internet using a 28Kbps modem, the file transfer will be much slower, limited by the speed (or lack of speed) of his modem.

You can modify the speed of the file transfer, as shown in **Figure** 2.22. This is especially useful when you are doing multiple, simultaneous file transfers. By moving the Speed indicator away from the Max speed, you can give greater priority (bandwidth) to your other file transfers. This will slow one transfer while speeding another.

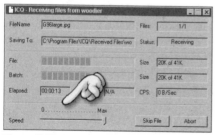

Figure 2.22 Select the speed you want to send or receive files.

What do I do when someone tries to send me a file?

You are alerted by ICQ when an incoming file request is received. ICQ then launches a long, but important, warning message telling you to be careful when receiving files because the file might contain viruses. The warning also suggests that you know the person who is sending the file. If you are satisfied that you know or trust the person sending you the file, click OK to continue with the file transfer. By checking the box on the bottom of this warning, you will not receive this message again.

A larger **Incoming File Request** window appears when the file transfer is started. This window contains information from the sender, such as his or her ICQ number, nickname, and e-mail address. You can also choose to review the user information by clicking the user information icon available on this window. The date and time of the file transfer are also provided for your information. Most importantly, information about the file is displayed, beginning with an optional description of the file, followed by the filename and file size.

On the lower part of the Incoming File Request window, you are provided with two respond actions and two receive actions.

Respond Actions

▶ **Send a message to the sender**—This keeps the File Transfer window open so that you can choose another response.

▶ **Decline**—You have different options to decline.

— Decline without giving a reason.

— Decline: "Sorry, I'm busy right now and cannot respond to your request."

— Decline: "Sorry, I'm busy right now, but I'll be able to respond to you later."

— Away: Reply with an away message.

— Enter a decline reason

Receive Actions

▶ **Save As**—Change the name of the file and the folder where you want it saved. Be careful that the file will not overwrite important files on your hard drive by having the same name.

▶ **Save**—The files will save in the default directory for the user sending you the file.

As in may other ICQ events, you have access to additional functions, which include Archive To, Create As Note, Mark As To Do, Add to Reminder, Print, and Delete All Incoming Events.

Selecting Close closes the Incoming File Request window and ignores the file transfer. No decline reason will be sent to the sender of the file.

The **Read Next** option allows you to review all pending events. By clicking the Read Next button, you can review each waiting event one by one.

 **Where does the file go on my computer after I've finished receiving it?**

If you're like us, two minutes after a file transfer, we have no idea where we put the file. Luckily, ICQ does some of your file organization for you. Where your file is stored on your hard drive after it has been received depends on the file Save option you chose when accepting the file transfer.

If you choose Save, the file is saved in the default folder. This is one of the most convenient ways to organize files. The default folder is a subfolder of the ICQ program containing the nickname of the person who sent you the file. Depending on where you chose to install ICQ, an example of a default folder might be C:\Program Files\ICQ\Received Files + the nickname of the contact who sent you the file. This folder will contain each file the user sends to you. Because filenames often are not very meaningful, this is a great way to keep files organized, at least by sender.

If you choose Save As, you were prompted to choose the folder in which to save the file. It's a good idea to keep only a single folder for incoming files, so that you know later where you can find the files you've received.

If you choose to organize your files differently, you are not stuck with selecting Save As each time or saving the files in the ICQ defaults. You can modify these settings by following these steps:

1. From the **ICQ window,** click the ICQ button to bring up the menu.

2. Select **Preferences & Security.**

3. Click **Preferences,** and the **Owner Prefs** For window appears.

4. On the **Accept** tab, type the path of the folder where you want files to be saved. Instead of typing the path and possibly getting it wrong, you can choose to browse your computer for the folder, and the path will be automatically entered for you. Click the small icon next to the path to browse for the folder.

5. Click **OK** to finish.

If you decide that you like the organization by contact, but you don't want the files saved in a folder beneath the ICQ folder, you can choose a different path, and ICQ will add directories as you receive files from contacts. Put a check mark in the check box labeled Save under user name folder.

The file path option is currently the only file transfer option you can configure. Click OK after you have entered the file path.

How can I view the file that was sent to me?

Receiving files through ICQ is a little like getting a present: You can't wait to see what's inside. When a file has completed downloading, you get a dialog box with three buttons (see **Figure 2.23**):

▶ **Goto Dir**—Opens the folder in which you saved the file.

▶ **Open**—The file is opened using the application that is assigned for the type of file you have received. For example, if someone sends me a JPEG graphics file, my computer opens the file using Paint Shop Pro, because this is the application Windows has assigned to open this type of file. You may have other applications assigned. If no application is assigned, Windows presents you with a list of possible applications and asks you to choose one. If you are unsure, do not select just any application, because the file may forever be associated with the wrong application.

▶ **OK**—Closes the File Receive window without viewing the file.

Figure 2.23 ICQ file transfer complete.

Using Windows Explorer (or some other file navigation utility, if you are using a different operating system), you have access to previously received files. You will need to know where on your hard drive they were saved. Browse your hard drive and find the place where you saved the file. Clicking on the filename will launch the application associated with the file type, allowing you to view the file.

If you know both the file type and the application that opens that file type, you can also choose to launch the application and then use **File > Open** from the application's menu to open the file. For example, if you've received a Word document, you can launch Microsoft Word and choose File > Open to open the document. You may have to use the browse feature to locate the file in the folder where it was saved.

Q45 Can people send viruses to me using ICQ?

Whenever a file is transferred across the Internet, there is a danger that it may contain a virus. This is no different from flying your favorite airline. Get on a plane, catch a cold. ICQ has no built-in ability to watch for viruses that files you receive using ICQ may contain. It's always a good idea to purchase and install the best virus checker (antivirus program) you can afford. Most antivirus software allows you to download a trial version. If you transfer files across the Internet, whether through ICQ or e-mail, or download them from Web pages, it's a good idea to scan them for viruses.

Not all virus transfers are done maliciously. Most people who send viruses have no idea they are sending them. Viruses often have the ability to attach themselves unseen to files and e-mail messages. Some will even e-mail themselves to everyone in your e-mail Contact List.

TIP

Be concerned about viruses, but not paranoid. There are as many (if not more) virus hoaxes on the Internet as there are viruses. I ignore all virus warnings that do not come from a recognized virus expert site, such as McAfee (**www.mcafee.com**) or Norton AntiVirus (**www.norton.com**). CNET's download site (**www.download.com**) also has the latest-breaking news on computer viruses.

When using the Internet, it's very important to have an antivirus program installed on your computer. Use these programs to check every file you receive for viruses before you open them. Antivirus programs are available from download sites similar to the one where you may have downloaded ICQ.

The **www.download.com** site has a virus news center that contains breaking news on the latest computer viruses and links to download the programs that detect and eliminate them.

All types and sizes of antivirus programs are available. Some antivirus programs specialize specifically in detecting viruses in e-mail, while others run all the time, detecting viruses in any file being loaded onto your computer no matter how it is being loaded, by ICQ or floppy disk.

Sending a URL

A URL, or Uniform Resource Locator, is the standard way to address resources on the Internet. A resource might be a Web page, FTP site, Real Media server, or some other file or application. Every URL on the Internet is unique, and there are literally billions of URLs. As you find interesting resources on the Internet, it's natural to want to share them with friends, family, and coworkers.

Section 2 Communicating

I've found the ultimate recipe site on the Web. How do I send the Web address to my friends on ICQ?

So many cool Web sites exist today that we can find almost everything we need know, from paper making to human cloning. It's easy to get excited about the interesting resources. For example, there are Web sites maintained by experienced chefs who instruct you on how to prepare an elegant dish. You can also find recipes for just about any type of food imaginable. When you come across a good recipe and want to share it with friends, rather than write out the whole recipe and copy it into an e-mail message or call people on the phone to share it with them, it's easier if you simply send the URL of the Web site to them through ICQ. To send a URL:

1. Click the nickname in your Contact List of the person you want to receive the URL.

2. When the menu pops up, click the **Web Page Address (URL)** option. Please note that URLs can be used to address many types of Internet resources, not just Web pages. ICQ will add the address of the Internet resource or Web page and, if available, will sometimes add a description automatically.

3. You can always change or add your own description. If you have more than one browser open, ICQ will enter the address of the browser you last accessed. You are given the option of typing in or changing the URL before it's sent.

4. Once the correct URL has been entered, click the **Send** button.

Q47

Should I send URLs to everyone in my Contact List each time I find a cool page?

You can send as many URLs as you like to as many people on your Contact List as you want. You can choose to send URLs to one of your contacts, to some of them, or to all of them. This question is not so much about the technical ability to send URLs as it is about Internet courtesy.

It's important that you consider the privacy of your friends and family in your Contact List. I'm sure they enjoy getting the occasional interesting URL. But, it's easy to get bombarded by many people on your list "sharing" with you. Not all Web pages are for all kinds of people. Be selective about the types of URLs you send to your contacts. So, it's probably not a great idea to send Grandma links to PunkLife (www.punklife.com) unless it's to buy you a BadReligion shirt for your twelfth birthday. Your environmentalist friends might not appreciate your fine-clothing suggestions from your favorite Internet furrier, www.getfur.com.

It's nice to get a URL every time something important or interesting arises, but it gets annoying after a while to receive URLs every two hours offering chain letters, soliciting better long-distance rates, or discussing friendship and love. No matter how many millions of ways to express friendship and love, the first involves respect. We feel strongly that you should not abuse ICQ by sending any type of unsolicited plea or advertisement.

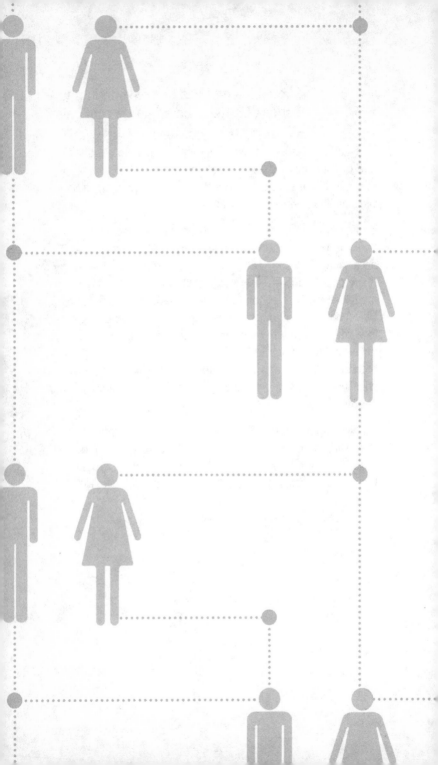

Section 3
Customizing ICQ

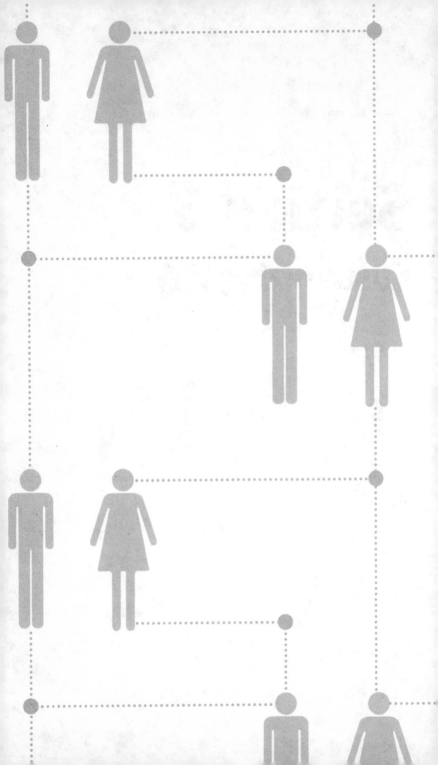

Customizing ICQ

Adding Users

The ICQ program is configurable to allow many users to use a single ICQ program. Each user can maintain a personal Contact List, user preferences, and history of ICQ events. You can also use this ability to have several of your own ICQ accounts. In this way, you can maintain both personal and business ICQ accounts.

 **Everyone in my family wants their own ICQ number. How do I add new users?**

It's uncommon for every member of the family to have their own computer. Most families share one or two computers at home. When they share computers, they also share the programs installed on them. Sharing ICQ is common, too, but each member of the family can have a personal ICQ number with individual contacts and history. This way, everyone can have privacy, and when you log in to your own ICQ account, you won't be bothered by messages from your family members' contacts. Only the contacts of the currently logged-in user will be notified of a user online event.

To add a new user for the same computer:

1. From the ICQ window, click the **My ICQ** button.
2. Select **Registration** to ICQ.
3. Click **Register a New User.**

Section 3   Customizing ICQ

4. Two windows pop up. The first window is a note from ICQ. Click **OK** to close this window. The second window is the ICQ Registration Window. You will have to go through the registration to get a new number (follow the steps in **Question 5**).

Once you register, ICQ will start with the new ICQ user number. It will be like starting ICQ for the first time. You can add as many users as you need or want. Just follow the preceding steps, and you are all set.

Creating new users also means creating a new identity. Every ICQ number will have its own Contact List and history and can be configured differently. You will have the same contacts only if you add them to your list under both ICQ numbers.

Now that every family member has an ICQ number, how do we switch users?

Privacy is not always about protecting your information from people on the Internet. Often, we like to keep our communications private, even in our own home. In **Question 48**, we talked about adding new users with completely separate identities to ICQ. If you haven't already done so, set up an ICQ account for each member of your family. Or, if you are using ICQ on a public computer at the office, set up an ICQ account for each office member. Then, when you're ready to use ICQ with your personal account, you simply change ICQ users, following these steps:

1. Click the **My ICQ** button on the ICQ window.
2. Select **Change User On This Computer**.
3. Choose **Change Active User**.
4. From the list, click your nickname and ICQ number.
5. ICQ will confirm that you want to make this change. Click **Yes**.

In the last step, ICQ asks if you want to bestow ownership. Don't be confused by this question. This has no bearing on who owns the ICQ program. When sharing the ICQ program with several people, you can think of it as more of a timeshare; when you're logged in, it belongs completely to you.

After you confirm that you want to bestow ownership on yourself, ICQ relaunches, logging in to the ICQ network using your ICQ number. The ICQ program is pretty smart and will restart in the same mode it was in the last time you used it. For example, if you were operating with the Invisible mode set and then changed users, when you return to your account, ICQ will once again be operating in Invisible mode.

If you want to keep your ICQ information truly private, be aware that asking ICQ to remember your password makes it possible for anyone to change to your ICQ account and read, change, or delete any of your information. If you consider this to be a possibility, we recommend that you remember your ICQ password and enter it each time you connect to the ICQ network.

A real dilemma you may confront is what to do after you finish using ICQ and want to bestow ownership on someone else, without leaving ICQ connected with your ICQ number. ICQ has no good mechanism built into it for this scenario, so you have to create a "dummy" user. This fictitious user does not have to have any contacts, but it could. In an office environment, this user could be the general office ICQ account that listens for incoming ICQ messages for the entire group. Switching to this user after you finish your personal ICQ session will protect your privacy and allow ICQ to be useful for the entire group. (Again, **Question 48** explains how to add a new user.) If you want your dummy user to have an e-mail address, you can always obtain a free e-mail address from one of the many services providing free e-mail accounts, including ICQ itself.

ICQ on Your Desktop

No matter how powerful a tool is, the simple fact remains that if the tool is not easy to access, you probably will not use it. Make things easy for yourself by making it simple to access ICQ. This section shows you some ways to streamline your ICQ access.

Do I have to have the ICQ program on my screen all the time?

There are many options available for configuring how the ICQ program appears on your desktop. Customizing these features will sometimes make the difference in how you feel about using the ICQ program. You generally leave ICQ running while working with other programs, but if you don't have the features set so that you are comfortable with it, the program will get in the way. You'll probably grow annoyed and shut it down, thus losing the power of instant messaging and all the other great ICQ features.

Sizing the ICQ window is everything

It takes a little playing with ICQ to find out what configuration will work best for you. Be patient and adjust the display settings as you prefer. Changing the shape and size of the ICQ window is the quickest way to change how ICQ appears on your screen. Moving your mouse over any of the outside edges of the ICQ window causes the mouse pointer to change to a double-ended arrow; this is known as the *resize* pointer.

With your mouse pointer positioned over the edge of the ICQ window and displayed as a resize pointer, click the left mouse button and drag the edge of the window until you are satisfied with the window's new height or width. Dragging from any of the four corners of the window simultaneously adjusts the height and width.

ICQ remembers the window size you select. Changing the active user, as described in **Question 49,** changes the size of the window to the size configured by that user.

Always on top

While running more than one program in Windows, keeping the windows organized can be a challenging task. Finding the ICQ window when you need it shouldn't add to your confusion. Configuring ICQ to always appear on top, no matter how many windows you have open, is one way to have ICQ at your fingertips. The ICQ window can remain onscreen all the time if you wish. This way, when you choose to operate in a mode other than Available/Connected, you can see when messages appear in your Contact List by the visual cue of the flashing message icon next to your contact's name. If you find that ready access to your Contact List is important to you, you'll want ICQ located where you can see it at all times.

Another way to have ICQ on top is to configure the ICQ window to appear whenever an incoming event is detected, such as an incoming message, URL, or chat request. The ICQ window will appear above any other open windows on your screen. Going one step further, you can also have the window disappear when you're not using it. In this case, the ICQ window automatically minimizes after a specified amount of time.

Customizing the window placement

Leaving the ICQ window minimized does not minimize its functionality. The tray icon, normally the lovely greenish flower, is an important way you can interact with the ICQ program. The icon will change and flash, letting you know when incoming events occur and when your own status changes. Remember that your status can automatically change to Away and Extended Away modes when you haven't typed or moved your mouse for a while.

Right-clicking the tray icon opens a menu of the more important ICQ services, preferences, and status-setting features. To access your Contact List, you need to open the ICQ window itself. You can access many of the other ICQ services directly from this menu. Therefore, operating with the ICQ window minimized can still give you instant access to ICQ. Even more personalized access to your Contact List is provided by a feature known as *floating*, discussed in **Question 51**. To configure the behavior and placement of the ICQ window, follow these steps:

1. Click the **ICQ button** in the ICQ window.

2. Click **Preferences**.

3. In the Preferences window, select **Contact List** from the menu on the left.

4. Customize your ICQ contact list behavior by checking the boxes in the **Options** tab.

Without the ICQ window on my screen, how do I know when my friends are online?

ICQ has a treasure trove of features available to alert you when your friends are online. After all, knowing when your contacts are online is really the killer feature of instant messaging generally, and ICQ specifically. Foremost is the ICQ Global Online Alert, which sounds like something the president might always carry around in a briefcase. Actually, it acts more like a party favor on your desktop, blinking and making noise. When your contacts come online, you will see the flower icon in the tray, accompanied by a little face (see **Figure 3.1**). Just as the sound of someone knocking on a wooden door always sends the dog running for the door to see who's there, the Global Online Alert will send you to your tray icon to see who has come online.

Figure 3.1 User is online.

How to make a "floating user"

Is there someone in your Contact List you want to keep a close eye on? If keeping the ICQ window on your screen isn't possible, or your Contact List is so large that scrolling through it to check the online status of your friends is tedious, you can "float" users. Your contacts can each appear outside the ICQ window in their own tiny status window, not much larger than the contact's name and icon. Simply click the contact's name and, while holding down the mouse button, drag the contact from the ICQ window onto your computer desktop. You can drag this floating contact to any portion of the screen you wish. We tend to keep our floating contacts along the top of our screen. Your floating contact will have all the same characteristics as the contact in the ICQ window. You can send messages, request chats, and see their online status change.

Another way to make a user "float" is to click your contact's nickname in the Contact List, select More (Rename, Delete...) from the menu, and then click "Floating" On. Your contact will appear outside your Contact List. Drag the contact to any place on your computer desktop.

Floating users are most useful if they are set up to be "always on top." Follow these next steps to configure this option:

1. Click the **ICQ button** in the ICQ window.
2. Click **Preferences.**
3. In the Preferences window, select **Contact List** from the menu on the left.
4. In the **Options** tab, the third option should be selected, so that floating users will not get lost behind windows.

The idea of having floating users is that you can see them at all times. We really can't think of a reason why you would ever want to turn this feature off.

Section 3   Customizing ICQ

Working with Sounds

Have you ever dreamed of having a talking computer like the one on *Star Trek?* You'd command "Locate the doctor" and the computer would respond in a gentle, familiar voice, "The doctor is no longer aboard the ship." Well, silly as it might sound, you can set up ICQ to give you that same kind of friendly audio feedback. ICQ can alert you to many types of events with its built-in sounds, or you can create your own custom sounds. With a little creativity, ICQ can take on quite a personality.

 **I work in an office—can I shut off the "Uh oh" sound so that it doesn't disturb others?**

As much as we love to hear the funny "Uh oh" sound, when swapping messages in an office environment, this sound can become a nuisance. There are many reasons why you might want to turn off the sound and rely only on ICQ's visual cues to incoming events.

Yes, you can turn off some or all the sounds ICQ makes. To turn off all the ICQ sounds, follow steps 1 through 4. To disable only some of the sounds, continue through step 7.

1. Click the **ICQ button** on the ICQ window.

2. Click **Preferences.**

3. In the Preferences window, choose the **Events** option. From this window you can configure all of the events. To turn off the ICQ sounds, select the **General** tab and uncheck the option labeled: Configure ICQ to play a sound upon receipt of an event.

4. To configure sounds for individual events, select the **Sounds** tab and select the sound, preview the sound, or disable the sound for each of the events in the list.

5. To reset all of the ICQ sounds you can select a **Sound Scheme** from the list of Sound Schemes. (Selecting No Sounds will also disable all ICQ event sounds.)

6. When you have finished customizing the sounds click the **Apply** button.

Table 3.1—Default Sound Schemes

Sound Scheme Settings	Description
ICQ Default	ICQ plays its default sound for each event.
My Settings	Enables you to choose to disable some of the events or change the sound file for a specific event. These sounds will play the same sound files for all of your contacts. To disable a sound, click the event name and then click the Disable button at the right side of your screen. To change the event sound file, click the Select button, browse through your computer for the sound you want, and then click Open.
No Sound	None of the events will make any sound.

 **Can I have ICQ make announcements in other languages?**

Si! Yes! Hai! Hear ICQ announcements and notifications in any language you speak. No matter how obscure the language may be, ICQ can speak your language. Essentially, ICQ is not much more than a trained parrot when it comes to the sounds that it makes. The best part is that you get to be the trainer.

The process of getting ICQ to speak other languages begins by downloading a new Sound Scheme in the language of your choice. These Sound Schemes were created by other ICQ users and then uploaded to the ICQ Web site. From Australian to Urdu, these Sound Schemes vary in quality. We recommend that you download and try them, installing the sounds you like best. You can even mix and match languages.

You can download the new language Sound Schemes from **www.icq.com/sounds/ICQ_in_Different_Languages.html**, as follows:

1. Select the **Sound Scheme** you'd like to install and click the link to begin the download.

2. In the **File** dialog window that appears, select a directory on your hard disk to store the Sound Scheme file.

3. Click the **ICQ button** on the ICQ window.

4. Click **Preferences** and choose the Events tab.

5. Select the **Sounds** tab.

6. Click the **Import** button on the Sound Schemes section of the window.

7. Find the Sound Scheme file on your hard drive and select it.

8. Preview the sounds by using the **Preview** button.

9. Click the **OK** button to save your new sounds.

10. Click **OK** again in the Preferences window to return to ICQ.

We recommend previewing the sounds you have loaded. After using ICQ for a while, your ear becomes trained to hear certain sounds and associate them with certain events. When you change these sounds, ICQ may feel foreign to you. Thus, it's a good idea to identify ahead of time what sounds are associated with which events.

You may like some or all the sounds in your Sound Scheme. You are not stuck with any sounds you don't care for. You can return to the default sounds, choose a new Sound Scheme, change individual sounds, and create your own sounds. Continue on to **Question 54** to learn how to create new language sounds and Sound Schemes.

Q54 I'm not fond of the default sounds. Can I change them?

Do you have an Aunt Magna with a voice like fingers on a blackboard? She may be a very nice lady, but getting beyond her voice makes spending afternoons with her a chore. Sound affects our mood and how we feel. Babies are comforted by a sound that resembles their mother's heart, children are exhilarated by the sound of the recess bell, and tears well up in our eyes when we hear the sound of the wedding march. Spend as much attention to configuring the ICQ sounds as you possibly can. It will really affect how you feel about your interactions with ICQ.

Sound Schemes

You can change some or all the sounds that ICQ makes. There are simple ways to do this, such as downloading and installing a new Sound Scheme, a complete set of ICQ sounds. Installing Sound Schemes is explained in **Question 53**, which discusses adding Sound Schemes in other languages. Find Sound Schemes in other languages or styles and install them by following the steps in the previous question. You can find Sound Schemes created by ICQ users at **www.icq.com/sounds**.

Beyond Sound Schemes

You are not limited to sounds recorded by other people to personalize your ICQ program. You can create your own sounds and configure ICQ to use them. Grab your microphone and get comfortable. You're about to become a recording star.

There are many programs you can use to record sounds, but your Windows program comes with one that is satisfactory for the job. From your Windows Start menu, select **Programs > Accessories > Entertainment > Sound Recorder.** The Sound Recorder program opens.

When you are ready to record a new sound, click the Record button in the Windows Sound Recorder (the button with a red dot on it). Windows immediately begins creating a digital recording that can be saved to your hard drive. Speak slowly and clearly into your microphone. As you speak, you can watch your voice pattern as it is displayed in the Sound Recorder, as shown in **Figure 3.2**.

Figure 3.2 Watch the sound of your voice as you record with Windows Sound Recorder.

If you don't see your voice displayed, you likely are having one of the following problems:

▶ The microphone is not plugged into the sound card or is not operating. Some microphones have On/Off switches. Make sure your microphone is turned on.

▶ The sound card is not installed or is installed and improperly configured. Check the Windows system configuration and the sound card's troubleshooting guide for more help.

▶ You are not speaking loud enough. You should not have to speak above your normal speaking tone when the microphone is within two inches of your mouth. Do not blow or spit into the microphone.

Notice that while you are recording, Sound Recorder is keeping track of the length of your recording. We advise you to keep your recordings brief. Most people do not want to listen to a long monologue (the same one, over and over) each time an ICQ event is triggered. Use the existing ICQ sounds as a guide. Some of the existing ICQ sounds simply say, "User is online" or "Incoming chat request."

You can say anything you like, with no limitations. You may choose to record sounds rather than your voice. A recording of your favorite dog barking may confuse your cat and scare away burglars when you receive ICQ messages. Our dogs run to the door each time they hear the sound of the "knock on the door".

You can replay your recordings in Sound Recorder and choose to record over an existing recording. The sound quality will not diminish by recording over your first or second effort. Once you have the recording you are happy with, choose File > Save from the Sound Recorder menu. ICQ has no requirement regarding where these files must be saved, but we recommend creating a folder beneath the ICQ folder for storing custom sounds. This will help you find them later and organize your files so that you can create your own Sound Schemes.

To add your new sound to ICQ, launch the **Owner Preferences** window, select **Events** from the menu on the left, and then select the **Sounds** tab.

After you associate your sound file with an event, you can click the **Preview** button to listen to your sound. When you finish configuring your sounds, click the **Apply** button.

I'd like special notification depending on who is online. Is there a way to set that up?

Imagine that every time one of your contacts comes online, you hear their voice saying "Hello, I am online." That kind of personalization can make you feel much closer to your contacts, as though they were only across the room. You can use recordings of the contact's voice to create special alert messages. This is the same technique used by radio stations when they have recordings of artists presenting their own song.

So far in this section, we have talked about how to set the **Global Online Alert** messages. These are the default messages you hear when any incoming event is detected by ICQ. You can also customize the sounds played for events based on each individual contact.

Personalizing sounds

Ask each of your contacts to record several sound files saying things like, "I'd like to chat with you" or "Here's a message." Use the ICQ File Transfer to have them send the sound files to you. Then, to play their personal greeting instead of the global default greeting:

1. From your **Contact List,** click the contact you want to personalize.

2. Click **Alert/Accept Modes.**

3. In the **Alert/Accept Settings** window, select the **Alert** tab.

From this tab, you can override the Global Online Alert for this user by checking the check box. You can further customize the way ICQ alerts you by checking or unchecking any of the other Alert options on this tab. You can also disable sounds for this user only by checking the list box labeled **Disable Sounds.**

We now get to the part where you can associate custom sounds on a user-by-user basis. Clicking the **Setup Personal User Sounds** button launches the **Sound Config** window for the user you've selected to customize. This window has two sections, as shown in **Figure 3.3**:

▶ **User Identification Sound**—Check the **User ID** box and select a sound file that identifies your contact, such as a sound file that says only his or her name. With this option selected, the sound file you specify is played either before or after the ICQ default sound. You will hear the name of your contact played together with the default sound file. For example, a sound file that says "Bob" will be played before the default "is online" so that you hear "Bob is online."

▶ **Incoming Events**—You can choose the sound file you want to hear for your contact for a specific event. This option requires only a single sound file.

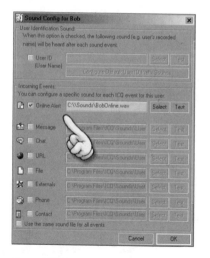

Figure 3.3 Choose the file you want to play for a specific event for this contact.

In any of the cases mentioned so far, to choose a sound file that you want to associate with your contact, click the **Select** button and browse your computer for the sound file you wish to use. After you find the file, click **Open.** You can preview the file you've chosen by clicking the **Test** button.

When you finish configuring the sounds for your contact, click the **OK** button.

The Aesthetic Touch

Art is in the eye of the beholder. Having already configured the way ICQ "talks" to you, it's now time to learn how to change ICQ's appearance. ICQ may not be the flashiest program in the world, but it's packed with functionality, and part of that functionality allows you to make it look pretty snazzy.

Q56 ICQ isn't the prettiest program. Can I make it look better?

What if you could just peel off your skin and take on a whole new look? You would still know all the same things and have the same abilities, but you'd look different. There are add-on programs that allow you to do just that—add a new *skin*, an alternative graphical interface, to ICQ, thus changing the way ICQ looks.

ICQ Plus is an add-on program for ICQ that makes it possible to easily pop on a new skin whenever you want to remodel the way your ICQ appears. You can have pictures of your friends, your kids, fantasy models, palm trees, or whatever you'd like to see when you look at ICQ. This program was written by Vadim Eremeev of St. Petersburg, Russia, and is offered free of charge.

With ICQ Plus, you can remodel the look of your ICQ completely. ICQ Plus allows you to apply skins that are composed of one or more images saved in JPEG format. ICQ Plus is just one of several skin programs available. There are skin programs available for Internet browsers, calculators, note pads, audio programs, and even for Windows itself.

You can download ICQ Plus from **www.download.com** or **www.tucows.com**. ICQ Plus is distributed as freeware and is updated constantly. You can find more information about this program at **www.icqplus.da.ru**.

You have to download this program and install it on your computer before you can use it. Its file size is about 1.6MB, and it installs fast and easily.

CAUTION

We have experienced odd ICQ behavior after installing this program. There was nothing fatal nor a reason not to install it. If you notice strange behavior after installing ICQ Plus, you can always choose to uninstall it.

After I add a new skin to enhance the look of my ICQ program, can I change it?

Your artistic sense can now go wild. You can download hundreds or thousands of skins and switch them whenever you feel the need for a little change on your desktop. Remember, changing the skin will not change the way ICQ operates. Also, some programs will radically change the shape of the program. ICQ Plus leaves ICQ the same size and shape that you have configured it.

To change ICQ skins (after ICQ Plus has been installed), click the small yellow plus sign at the top of your ICQ window. This opens a new window in which you can preview and select the skin you want to load. ICQ Plus comes with three demo skins. Click twice on the skin you want to use to load it.

Section 3   Customizing ICQ

NOTE

ICQ Plus installs itself as an add-on to your ICQ program. You can access the ICQ Plus menu by clicking the small plus sign on the ICQ window (see **Figure 3.4**). ICQ Plus also adds itself into Windows programs that are accessible from your Windows Start menu. Running ICQ Plus from the Start menu will not have any effect. You can access the functionality of ICQ Plus only from within ICQ.

Figure 3.4 The plus sign on your Contact List gives you access to the ICQ Plus program.

New skin

You also can create your own skins with your own images by editing the demo skins that come with the ICQ Plus program. The process for creating new skins is beyond the scope of this book. We will simply tell you that your images must be saved in JPEG format and must be 600 pixels high and 300 pixels wide to avoid appearing deformed.

Replace the images that come with the demo image, and watch how the image appears to be pasted on the face of your ICQ windows. Be careful to select light font colors in your Contact List when using an image with dark colors as a skin.

Configuring ICQ Plus

You can configure what you want to happen when you click the ICQ Plus sign. To see and configure all the options of your ICQ Plus program, click the ICQ button on the ICQ window and click the new option called Plus. The ICQ Plus window appears. From this window, you can completely customize ICQ Plus, changing skins as well as ICQ Plus's behavior. You can even have ICQ Plus load a random skin each time ICQ launches.

To add a new skin, follow these directions:

1. Click the **Import** button in the ICQ Plus window.

2. Browse in your computer for the Zip file that contains the new skin. ICQ Plus will copy the files to its own folders. After a few seconds, you will see the new skin in the ICQ Plus window.

3. Click **Apply** and the ICQ window will change to the new skin. Once you're done, click **OK.**

Q58 Where can I go to find new skins?

One of the great things about the Internet is that it never takes long for a great thing to catch on. Some very creative people have been busy creating thousands of skins that work with ICQ Plus. **Table 3.3** lists just a few of the many places you can surf on the Web to find new skins. Remember that you also can create your own skins and upload them to these sites for others to use.

Table 3.3—Sites Offering Skins

Site Name	Site Address
Skinz.org (see **Figure 3.5**)	**www.skinz.org**
TUCOWS Free Themes	**www.freethemes.com**
EZskins	**www.ezskins.com**
My Screens	**www.myscreens.com**
ICQ Skins by Blue Genie 2	**www.crosswinds.net/ ~bluegenie2/skins.html**

NOTE
All the skins you download must be in a Zip file.

Figure 3.5 The Chinese Man 2K skin, downloaded from www.skinz.org.

You can also get more information about skins on the ICQ Cool Links page at **www.icq.com/coollinks/** or at the ICQ Plus site. If you'd like to know more about adding a new skin, refer to **Question 57.**

I don't want to install more programs in my computer. Is there a way to change the color without using skins?

You can configure your ICQ window with your favorite colors. You can change the color of your online contacts, offline contacts, contacts waiting for authorization, future users, users not listed, Web users, group names, links, and the background. There are no limits on which colors you can choose; you can use one of the preselected colors or define your own colors.

To customize the colors, click the **ICQ button** and then click **Preferences.** In the **Owners Preferences** window, select **Contact** List from the menu on the left and then select the **Colors** tab.

You are next shown a list of the many different types of contacts and the color set for each contact type. To change colors, click the color you want to change, and a new window will open. You can choose from forty Basic Colors or sixteen Custom Colors that you can define by clicking the Define Custom Color button. Select the color from the color picker and click the **Add to Custom Colors** button. This new color will appear in one of the bottom boxes. Select the custom color and click **OK.** You will return to the Colors Window. When you have completed customizing the colors for your Contact List, click **Save.**

Configuring Security and Privacy

Of concern to anyone accessing the Internet, both security and privacy are important issues when choosing to use the ICQ program. ICQ, by design, is capable of revealing a great deal of information about you and your Internet connection. You can choose to remain completely anonymous or freely distribute your personal information. This is not an area you want to ignore.

 **I don't want just anyone having access to my information. How can I protect it?**

There is no good way to protect all of your personal information when using ICQ. You do have some control over the information that you allow others to see. The best way to protect your private and personal information is not to enter the information into ICQ. You are free to share the information with people as you become acquainted with them.

TIP

We recommend that you enter a nickname so that your contacts will easily be able to identify you when they receive messages or other events from you.

Your user information

ICQ does allow you to enter a great deal of information about yourself, including a map to your house. By configuring the ICQ security and privacy settings, you can limit to whom and when your personal information is released. For example, when you first installed ICQ, you likely were hoping both to make new friends based on your location or interests and to reconnect with "lost" friends and family. You diligently entered every piece of information you could recall about yourself, making it as easy as possible for others to find you.

Now, after having hundreds of people wondering whether you know what happened to Judy Smith, the girl they all loved in high school, because your name happens to be Paul Smith, you're ready to begin limiting which information people see. You may even want to completely hide your details. Follow these steps:

1. Click the **ICQ button** on the ICQ window.

2. Click **View/Change My Details.** The ICQ Global Directory— My Details window will open.

3. Click the button at the bottom labeled **More Options.** Then select **Unlist** from the menu.

4. Click **Yes** or **No,** depending on whether or not you want to follow the ICQ advice. If you choose to delete the details about yourself, only the information you choose to retain will be available for others to see.

Your primary e-mail address

Some people are hesitant to release their primary e-mail address because of the large number of unscrupulous Internet mass marketers. You can choose to hide this address while still supplying it to ICQ so that if you forget your password, ICQ can e-mail it to you. Remember that the e-mail address you entered when you first registered is the only place ICQ will send your password. To hide your primary e-mail address:

1. Click the **ICQ button** on the ICQ window.

2. Choose **View/Change My Details.** This launches the ICQ Global Directory—My Details window.

3. Select your primary Email address from the list and click the **Edit** button. A new window will open.

Section 3 Customizing ICQ

4. In this window, check the box labeled **Don't publish my Primary email address, use it for password retrieval purposes,** and click **OK.** Once this is checked, your primary e-mail address will not be available to others. Remember that this option does not keep secondary e-mail addresses from being available to the public. To keep people from seeing these addresses, you must remove them.

Your photo and phone number

From the same ICQ Global Directory—My Details window, but on either the Picture tab or Phone—Follow Me tab, you can select to send your picture or phone number to all users or only to users in your Contact List, show a request for a picture or phone, and make it impossible for others to see your picture or phone number. When you finish configuring all of your information, click Save.

I use ICQ on a public computer at the local cyber café. Can anyone use my ICQ account?

Cyber cafés are springing up everywhere. If you travel, you may find yourself needing a cyber fix and a cup of coffee. Almost all cyber cafés now have ICQ installed, making it easy for you to stay in touch with your ICQ friends and family. Add yourself as a registered user and log in to the ICQ network, and it's just like being at home. Almost...

Yes, actually everybody can use your ICQ number if you've added yourself as a user on a public computer without adding a password. If you find yourself going to the same cyber café and sitting at the same computer all the time, and don't want to go through the hassle of adding yourself as a registered user each time and then deleting your account each time when you're done, we recommend you protect your ICQ with a password. Don't select the option to have ICQ remember your password; otherwise, it's like not having a password at all.

TIP

If you are going to different cyber cafés or are not always using the same computer, you should uninstall your ICQ account from that computer when you finish using it. That way, no record of your ICQ number will be available, so no one will try to hack your password.

Please use extra caution when using your ICQ account on a public computer. We'd like to think that everyone on the ICQ networks is wonderful. Sadly, that's just not the case. To protect your ICQ with a password:

1. Click the **ICQ button** on the ICQ window.

2. Click **Security & Privacy.** On the Security tab of the Security dialog box (see **Figure 3.6**), you will see a section called **Security Level.** Since you are going to be in a place where you don't know who could use your ICQ number, you should select the radio button for High. This way, no matter who attempts to start ICQ using your number, they will be prompted for a password. Remember your password and don't give it away to anyone.

3. Click **Save.**

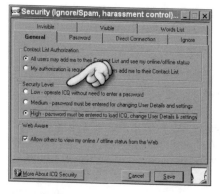

Figure 3.6 Choosing the highest level of security will prevent others from launching ICQ using your ICQ number without entering your password.

CAUTION

When you add your ICQ number to a computer that either isn't yours or is shared with others, it's very important that you use at least a Medium security level.

The ultimate protection when using your ICQ number on public computers is to remove your account when you are finished for the day. To uninstall an ICQ account from a computer:

1. Click the **My ICQ** button on the ICQ window.

2. Change **User In This Computer.**

3. Select **Remove ICQ# from Computer.**

4. Click the ICQ number you want to remove.

5. Enter your password.

6. Click **Next.**

7. The first warning will appear, telling you that you are about to delete a user from the computer. Don't let that scare you. You can reregister on that computer at any time.

8. Click the radio button labeled **Yes, please remove me.**

9. Click **Next.**

10. A second warning dialog will appear, making sure you want to delete that number. Click **OK,** and the ICQ number will be deleted from that computer.

We thought we'd end this section by quoting from the ICQ help files under New Features in ICQ 99b: "Please note: The ICQ features described in this help file may not operate according to the description provided herein or may not operate at all, including privacy and security features." Consider this a warning. When things don't operate quite as you'd expect, refer to this quote!

Section 4
All the Goodies

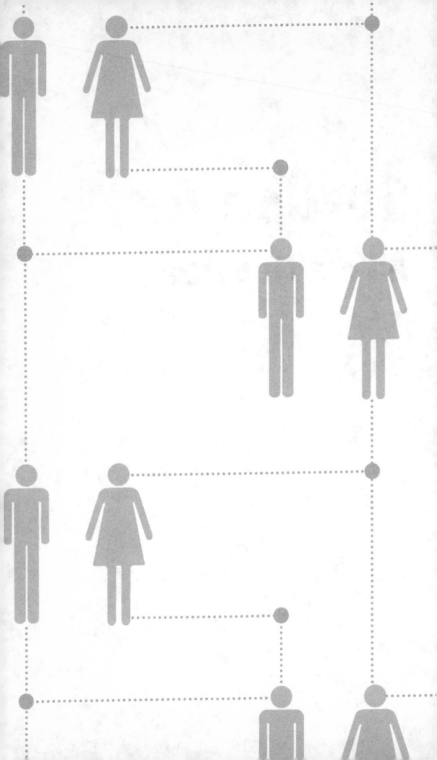

All the Goodies

We said at the beginning of the book that ICQ was a full-featured personal and business management tool. It has features that rival any business communications and contact management tool, such as its contact management and communications capability (covered in the first three sections).

Personal Homepage

The World Wide Web has become a global community where people share information about themselves, transact business, communicate, and play. There's never been a resort, anywhere in the world, that offers so much for such a low price! ICQ enables you to be a part of that community, not only as a communicator, but also as a participating member on the Web.

Web pages are simply documents, identified with a special address known as a Uniform Resource Locator (URL). A URL contains information about what machine will provide that document and whether the document will be provided using the Web. URLs that begin with HTTP or HTTPS contact a program known as a *Web server*. The next part of the URL, www.*someserver*.com, identifies the machine (*someserver*) running the Web server software. If no document name is specified, the Web server knows to send the default document, also known as a Web page. If a filename is included after the name of the machine, such as

http://www.someserver.com/mypage.html

the Web server located at www.*someserver*.com will send the file mypage.html. You will notice that many documents on the Internet have special file extensions, such as .html, .htm, .asp, or .xml. These are documents (pages) that are specially formatted to be read in a Web browser, such as Netscape Navigator or Microsoft Internet Explorer. These documents contain codes that let the browser know how to format the page and, in some cases, run small programs that are embedded in the pages.

This section will help you create a Web page and make it available to others over the Web by using your ICQ program.

Do I have to be a Web programmer to create my own ICQ homepage?

Creating a Web page is as simple as creating a word processing document in a program such as Microsoft Word or one of the other popular word processing programs. You can create informative, fun, and colorful Web pages that include photos and even sounds, with no programming whatsoever. Just as with Microsoft Word, you also have the ability to add more complex features that require you to delve deeper and understand some of the underlying technology.

All of the ICQ homepage features are available by clicking the **Services** button on the ICQ window and selecting **My ICQ Web Front**. To get started building your homepage, select **Customize My ICQ Web Front**. This launches the ICQ Web Front window.

ICQ Web Front

Homepage is a term that was coined as part of the Web. A homepage refers to a personal or default Web page. Remember that a Web page is a document that you create and publish over the Internet through a Web server. There is nothing about a homepage that distinguishes it from any other kind of page on the Web. It just usually refers to the first page someone sees when they access your Web site. It is sometimes referred as the "top page" because it acts as the entry point to any other pages you publish.

ICQ provides a very nice tool, called the **Homepage Factory,** to help you design and construct a Web page. By using each of the features in the Homepage Factory, you will end up with a nicely constructed Web page. For people who already have Web page experience, the Homepage Factory will let you get in and work at the HTML level. We'll also provide a few of HTML basics here so that you can understand what you're looking at in the Homepage Factory.

CAUTION

In versions of ICQ prior to 2000a there was a hole where hackers could get into someone's computer and download files. This hole was created whenever ICQ users activated their ICQ Web Front (ICQ Homepage factory for early versions). Through this security hole, any person could access important files on your computer, such as the win.ini file, change files or wreak malicious demage. As ICQ has evolved, so have the programs used to exploit security holes. We recommend being over-cautious when using the Homepage or Web Front feature. If you see anything unusual happening on your computer, immediately stop using the ICQ Web Front.

The Homepage Factory has three tabs: **Main, Design,** and
Advanced. The Main tab appears when you launch this
program, and it's a great place to get started. The Main tab
contains two windows (see **Figure 4.1**): the **Homepage
Modules** window, and a window that contains the name of
whichever module is being edited. For example, when the
Home module is selected in the Homepage Modules window,
the title of this second window is Home. The *modules* are
portions of your page that you can customize.

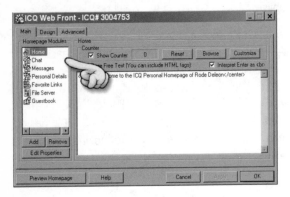

Figure 4.1 Begin by clicking the Home module.

A Short Guide to Web Page Programming

Web pages are primarily made up of text and pictures
(graphics). The text displayed on a Web page can be
formatted so that when it appears in a Web browser,
such as Netscape Navigator or Internet Explorer,
others will view it as you have designed it. To format
the page, special codes are inserted into the page
that affect how the page appears. These codes are
called *markup tags.* The unique thing about Web
pages is that you can include a special markup tag,
called a *hyperlink* (or *link* for short) that contains the

URL of another page. The links are clickable, and clicking a link loads the page specified by the URL in the tag. Most other tags relate either to formatting the way text appears or inserting images into the page. So, the group of tags is called the *Hypertext Markup Language (HTML)*.

HTML tags begin with a less than sign (<) and end with a greater than sign (>). For example, the tag that tells the Web browser to begin a new line is <BR>. This stands for BREAK, for line break. Some tags that mark the beginning of a text change also have an associated end tag. For example, the <B> that begins bolding text has an associated </B> end-bold tag. Notice that the end tag merely includes a / to distinguish it from the beginning tag. You can center text on the screen by using the <CENTER> tag, and have the text appear as a bold heading by using the <H1> through <H6> tags, which represent various heading levels and styles.

You can style your text by using <B> for bold, <I> for italics, and <U> for underline, along with their associated end tags. You already know that <BR> is a line break and thus has no end tag. You can begin and end paragraphs by using <P> and </P>. Add a horizontal line with the <HR> horizontal rule tag. This has no end tag either. You can get fancy with your fonts by using the <FONT> and </FONT> tag. This tag has a few more features. For instance, you can tell Web browsers what font you want to display text in. <FONT face=Arial> tells Web browsers to display the text using Arial font. Change text sizes by using the size parameter <FONT size=5>.

Some of the advanced tags are those used for graphics and hyperlinks. To put a picture in the page, use the image tag <IMG SRC="*mypicture.gif*">. The image (<IMG>) tag needs to know where the source (SRC) of the graphic can be found. Replace *mypicture.gif* in this example <IMG> tag with the name of the image you want displayed and place that tag in the page where you want the image to appear. Hyperlinks use the anchor tag (<A>):

```
<A HREF="http://www.someserver.com">this is a
link</A>.
```

Anchor tags have a beginning (<A>) and ending tag (</A>). When used for hyperlinking, they require the HREF value to contain the URL that is loaded when the hyperlink is clicked. The text that appears between the beginning and ending anchor tags will appear as a clickable link in a Web page. You can also replace the text with an image and therefore load a new page when the image is clicked.

Most Web servers and browsers require that pages have a file extension that the server or browser can associate with a Web document, such as .html, .htm, (HyperText Markup Language), asp (Active Server Pages), .xml (eXtended Markup Language), or .css (Cascading Style Sheet). If you are writing simple HTML, your file will have either the .html or .htm file extension. When a file is requested that the Web server does not recognize as a Web file, the file is sent to the browser using file download. This is how files are downloaded from the Web.

Main tab

Within the Homepage Modules, you will see a list of seven default modules (refer to **Figure 4.1**). We will describe each of these modules, with examples of how each can be modified to customize your Web page. Begin by clicking the module named Home. In the Home window to the right, you will see some text that looks like this:

```
<center>Welcome to the ICQ Personal Homepage of
</center>
```

The first thing you might notice is that this text starts and ends with the <CENTER> </CENTER> tag. Web browsers aren't picky about the case of the tags. They can be typed in either upper or lower case. Please refer to the sidebar "A Short Guide to Web Page Programming" for more information about HTML tags. The text displayed here will appear at the top of your page, centered on the page. Notice that it is missing your name at the end. You can choose to add your name as follows:

```
<center>Welcome to the ICQ Personal Homepage
of Freddy</center>
```

Or, you can choose to create a completely different top of the page, like this:

```
<center><B>I'm bold and you know it. Enjoy my
page.</B></center>
```

Notice that in the second example, we added the beginning and ending bold tags, <B> and </B>. The text will now appear centered and bold. You see how you can keep adding tags to change the way text is displayed. Here is text that is bold, underlined, italicized, centered, and in a different font style from the default (which happens to be Times New Roman in most Web browsers):

```
<CENTER><B><I><U><FONT face=Arial>This is some
text.</FONT></U></I></B></CENTER>
```

Use the tools you've learned about HTML and try adding your own text. Don't worry about breaking anything. You can always come back and change it if you are unhappy with it. **Figure 4.2** gives you an idea of how someone might display pictures of their cat and dog with a short introduction.

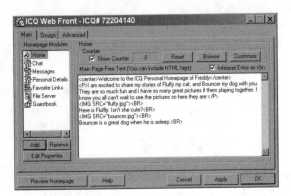

Figure 4.2 Fluffy and Bouncer find their way to cyber-immortality.

Before we move on to the next module, you can add a title to this section of your Web page. Click the Edit Properties button with the module highlighted. Enter the name you want to appear on your Web page for this section, and select an icon that people can click to take them to this part of your page. You can also personalize the font, color, and size of this section title.

TIP

You may want to click the Apply button once in a while to save your work as you continue modifying your Web page.

Next, click the Chat module in the window on the left of the Homepage Factory. The text in the window to the right will change, and the title of the window will change to Chat. This section represents the information you'd like to give to visitors of your page to convince them to chat with you. By default, the message is as follows:

If I'm currently online you can send me a chat request directly to my ICQ window. If I am available I will accept the request and the chat will begin!

Boring! Let's see if we can fix that up a little. Let's start with a snazzier message:

```
<FONT face=Arial size=6 color=blue>Text Me!</FONT>
<P>If I'm there, I'll chat with you.</P>
```

Okay, it's not a lot less boring. Notice that we've used the <FONT> tag to get a little attention to the Text Me! line. Then, instead of making the visitor read tons of text, keep the message short and separated into its own paragraph. Many people get excited about the Web, and the author in them emerges. We know from experience! But, unless you're publishing a magazine or writing an online book, most people have a short attention span while surfing the Web and appreciate short and to-the-point text on a page.

Experiment with some of the other HTML tags. There are many online HTML tutorials. Search Yahoo! (**www.yahoo.com**/) using the keyword HTML. Have fun and get a little crazy. You can always see what your page looks like as you are building it: click the Apply button to save your changes and then click the Preview Homepage button. Your new Web page will load in your Web browser.

The other modules you can customize are as follows (refer to **Figure 4.1**):

▶ **Messages**—Entice people to use the ICQ Web utilities on your page to send a message directly to your ICQ. Use HTML to make this request to your visitors to communicate with you exciting.

▶ **Personal Details**—Add a picture of yourself by checking Add User's Picture and selecting a picture from your hard drive. You will not need to use HTML for this. Also, any user information you have entered into ICQ will be displayed on your Web page. People will not have to get your permission to view this information.

▶ **Favorite Links**—Add the URLs of any of the Web pages you want to share with others. To add new links, use the anchor tag, discussed previously in the sidebar, "A Short Guide to Web Page Programming."

▶ **File Server**—Allow people to download files directly from your hard drive. You may choose to put files in a publicly accessible area or give people a password so that they can enter private areas of your computer. This is often useful in business situations, enabling you to distribute important files to others over the Internet.

▶ **Guestbook**—People can choose to leave you brief messages while visiting your Web page. This is a nice feature if you don't happen to be around to chat with them.

Design tab

Once you have the content on your page by entering it in the Home tab, click the **Design** tab of the Homepage Factory to further customize your homepage. **Figure 4.3** shows the Design tab selections. Change your homepage heading or remove it from the page. This is the graphic that appears at the top of your homepage. Customize the **Online Status Indicator** or choose to remove it from your page altogether. The Online Status Indicator lets people know when you're online and available. Remember that no one can view your homepage unless you're connected to the ICQ network. You can also design the colors for your page.

If you have the color sense of your pet dog (dogs are thought to be colorblind), then you can choose to use the ready-made **ICQ Factory Schemes.** There are five built-in factory schemes for you to choose from. Try them all. You can also click the button labeled **Click Here for More Schemes.** As of this writing, eight new schemes can be found at **www.icq.com/hpf/down.html.**

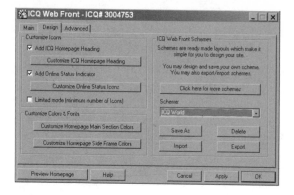

Figure 4.3 Change icons and color schemes in the Design tab.

Advanced tab

When you're finished, preview your homepage by clicking the **Preview Homepage** button along the bottom of your Homepage Factory. Your page will launch in a Web browser. Try clicking the icons along the left side of your page to visit the different areas that you've configured. Go back and change any areas that you don't like, or enhance the parts you do like. Your homepage can be a life project. To see how young you can start, visit **www.oceancoombs.com**.

Q63   Where does my homepage live?

ICQ provides you the ability to have two different homepages. When ICQ first started offering Web pages, it provided the service from the ICQ Web server. Everyone who has an ICQ number has one of these pages. Many of the ICQ features are available from this Web page. People can send you messages, chat with you, even see your online status. Your basic ICQ homepage URL is wwp.icq.com/your ICQ number here.

The second type of Web page ICQ provides you is unique. You may have heard that when you create a homepage, you have to upload it to a server so that others can view it. ICQ has a special built-in Web server that enables your homepage to be visible right from your computer when you're online and connected to the Internet. This is the homepage you build using the ICQ Web Front. (See **Question 62** for more information on the ICQ Web Front.)

You can modify your homepage file using the Homepage Factory. Even though the files for your homepage are located on your hard drive, they are in a format that only ICQ can interpret. You can create new pages that you link to from your ICQ homepage.

NOTE

The homepage files are located in C:\Program Files\ICQ\Homepage\Common\system. Remember that it's best to modify these files only with the Homepage Factory.

If you are feeling confident about your Web-page-building skills, or simply want to practice, try building Web pages that you can link to your ICQ homepage. Use Notepad or a Web-page-building program to create and modify these new Web files. The new files need to be stored in a special directory on your hard drive. Launch the Homepage Factory and select the **Advanced** tab. Then, click the **Open User Personal HTML Folder** button. This launches an Explorer window (see **Figure 4.4**) and displays the folder for storing your new Web pages. Notice the two default folders, files and images. The path to your files in the Explorer window is C:\Program Files\ICQ\Homepage\Root*your ICQ number*\personal. Your path will appear slightly different depending on both the drive letter assigned to the drive where you installed ICQ and your personal ICQ number. Note this path, because you need to know it to save and access files using programs for editing Web pages.

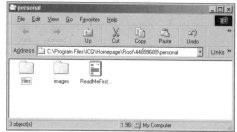

Figure 4.4 Access your personal homepage files directly on your hard drive.

Save new files into this folder by adding a filename such as this: C:\ProgramFiles\ICQ\Homepage\Root*your ICQ number*\personal\mypage.html.

After you create the files, you can link them into your homepage by using the Homepage Factory. Launch the Homepage Factory and, in the Main tab, select **Favorite Links.** Click the **Add Link** button.

Take a look at **Figure 4.5**, which shows the **Add New Link** dialog box. In the URL text field, enter the name of your file. If http:// is already in the text field, erase it before entering the name of your file. The http:// is there only to add links to files on other servers, such as http://www.yahoo.com.

Figure 4.5 Add a link to your new file.

Next, enter a title for your new Web page. Lastly, enter a description of your page. The title and description are displayed in the list of favorite links on your homepage. Create as many new pages as you like, linking them to your homepage in this manner.

Is it dangerous to have a homepage on my computer?

There is nothing inherently dangerous about having your homepage on your computer. The new version of ICQ solved some security issues apparent in earlier versions. However, you need to keep a few things in mind. Visitors to your homepage will know your IP address, which uniquely identifies your computer on the Internet. This is not really dangerous, but it is the information that a sophisticated hacker needs to exploit any security holes that might exist on your computer. The chances that a sophisticated hacker would want to break into your home PC are most likely slim to none. A sophisticated hacker is interested in high-profile or high-dollar-value hacks (computer break-ins). Letting people know your IP address is a little like putting your name, address, and telephone number in the phone book. With this information alone, someone could assume your identity, charge calls to your phone number, and play general havoc with your life. But, as with computer hacking on this scale, it rarely happens.

A bigger concern with hosting your own homepage is its popularity and the speed of your Internet connection. If you connect to the Internet over a normal dial-up modem, where your modem uses a telephone line to call an access number, you may want to reconsider hosting your own homepage, because when you check your e-mail, view Web pages, download files, ICQ chat, send ICQ messages, and perform other common Internet functions, you must move that information (data) across your Internet connection. You can think of that connection as a hose through which information can flow in both directions. This hose, your connection, has a certain capacity to transfer data. Dial-up modems have a fairly limited capacity. People accessing a homepage located on your computer will use some of that capacity to view your page. The more popular you become, the more people who will view your page, eating up your capacity (bandwidth). It's possible that even with very few people accessing your page, your own ability to do things that require a great deal of bandwidth (like transferring files) may become impaired.

Can I protect my homepage with a password?

Homepages are fun to share with friends and family. The things you share on your page are often personal and sometimes only of interest to those who know and love you. ICQ lets you protect your homepage with a password. Anyone trying to visit your page will be prompted to enter the password before being allowed to view the homepage.

To password-protect your homepage, start the ICQ Web Front and select the Advanced tab. Clicking the **Protect the Homepage with Password** button launches a small window in which you are asked to fill in a user ID and password. The choice for both the user ID and password are completely up to you.

CAUTION

The user ID and password that you choose to protect your homepage should not be the same as your ICQ nickname and password. This would require you to give out your secret password to others. In fact, the password should not be the same as any of your personal and private passwords. Choose something new.

I'd like to know who has been visiting my page. Is there a way to find out?

One of the really fun things about having a Web page is keeping track of how many people visit the page. ICQ keeps track of who visits your page and how many times they visit. **Figure 4.6** shows an example list of visitors. Unfortunately, you really don't get to know who it was that visited unless you know their IP address. Visitors are tracked by IP address and not by ICQ number.

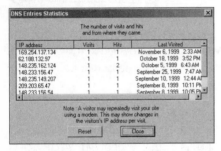

Figure 4.6 See who has been visiting your site.

To view the statistics of your Web page visitors, launch the Homepage Factory as follows:

1. Click the **Services** button on the ICQ window.

2. Select **My ICQ Web Front** from the menu.

3. Select **Customize My ICQ Web Front**. The ICQ Web Front will launch.

4. Click the **Advanced** tab. You will see an area of the Advanced tab labeled **Homepage Statistics,** which has two buttons.

5. Clicking **DNS Statistics** will give you the statistics shown in **Figure 4.6**. If you are interested in knowing when people visit your page most, click **Time Statistics**. The time statistics are useful for planning when you should be online making your ICQ homepage available. If you are connected all the time, then it's handy to know when the greatest amount of traffic is accessing your computer.

Reminders, Notes, and ToDo Lists

There was something we were supposed to write here, but we forgot what it was. Seriously, we all need a little help remembering things. ICQ has evolved into much more than simply a communicator—it is also a desktop personal organizer. Using many of the new features of ICQ, you can leave yourself electronic reminders, write notes, and set up ToDo lists.

 **When I'm on the Internet, I get so involved that I forget to do things. How can I have my computer prod me when I have things to remember?**

Have you ever noticed how time flies when you are surfing on the Internet? Sometimes, we even forget to do things such as walking the dog because we are so immersed in chatting with someone or visiting Web pages. If you don't live with your parents and are not married, there is nobody around to nag you. Yes, we are all responsible for our actions, but your mind can get sideways sometimes. The folks at Mirabilis (the makers of ICQ), knowing how cool it is to chat and surf the Internet, decided to create a utility that will send reminders. This is one of the many ICQ services that you can use even when you are offline.

Sometimes, you might get a message or see something mentioned in a chat for which you'd like to receive a reminder. You can make reminders out of messages, chats, or other events that are saved in the message archive.

To make new reminders:

1. Click the **My ICQ** button on the ICQ window.
2. **Select Reminder.**
3. Click **New Reminder.** The Add Reminder window will open.
4. Write the reminder on the bottom of the screen under Reminder Note. You will see that you can trigger this reminder in two ways: by selecting a day and time, or by specifying that it should be triggered when your contact comes online or comes back from Away or N/A mode. You can select any contact from your list to trigger this reminder.
5. To finish, click **Add to Reminder.**

You can also have a reminder prewritten, so that you won't have to rewrite the same reminder you use regularly. For example, if you normally go online around 6 p.m. and you want a reminder at 8 p.m. that the dog needs to be taken for a walk, you can reuse the reminder.

From the Add Reminder window, click the **Select Pre-set Reminder Note** button, which opens a list. Then, click Edit at the bottom of the list, which opens a new window called **Edit Reminder Preset.**

TIP
You can rename the label so that the name will be more meaningful to you. Click the Rename Label button, enter the new name, and click Save.

Write the reminder on the bottom of the screen under Preset Action Description. This will be the reminder that will appear at the time you specify. When you're finished, click Save.

To use this prewritten reminder, again click the **Select Preset Reminder Note,** and you will see the name of your reminder. Click the name, select how you want the reminder triggered, and click the **Add To Reminder** button. Remember, you can have the reminder triggered by time or event.

When the reminder is triggered, a window pops up on your screen, telling you how it was triggered, either by the time or by a contact event (see **Figure 4.7**). You have the option to either dismiss the reminder or have ICQ remind you again. Select a reminder option from the drop-down list to choose when you want to receive the reminder again.

Figure 4.7 Time to take the dog for a walk.

 **My computer monitor is covered with little yellow sticky notes that keep falling on my keyboard. Is there a better way to keep notes?**

If your desk looks like ours, your phone, computer monitor, and desktop are covered with yellow Post It™ notes. Now, ICQ offers a way to clean up your desk and monitor and organize your yellow "stickies" electronically. They are still small and yellow, but the best part is that they won't fall on your keyboard.

In a future not far off, we'll probably forget how to use a pen and forget what blank paper looks like. With smaller and faster PCs, rather than pull out a pen and paper to jot down a note, we'll turn to the computer. We also have seen some advances in speech-to-text software that convince us that it's only a matter of time until our fingers drop off from lack of use. But until the future arrives, there is an intermediate step you can take: Use the **ICQ Note Assistant** to take notes and keep them where they are easily accessed. This is one of the ICQ features that you can use even when you are offline. To use the ICQ Note Assistant, follow these steps:

1. Click **My ICQ** button on your ICQ window.

2. Select **Notes.**

3 The Notes window launches, from which you can choose the following:

> ▶ **New Note**—Click to create a new note. A little window opens with the date, for you to start writing your note.

> ▶ **Open Note List**—Click to open the Message Archive window in the Notes section. All the notes that you have saved are located there. Double-clicking the name of the note causes the entire note to appear.

> ▶ **Open**—Choose to open either all the notes or a selected note.

> ▶ **Close**—Close all the notes or only one note.

> ▶ **Bring All To Front**—Any notes that you have open will pop to the front so that you can see them.

Figure 4.8 shows how you can creatively format your notes to highlight certain notes or use them as a tree-friendly replacement for doodling on paper. You'll never get bored with these notes! When you have an open note, right-clicking the note enables you to choose from the following menu options:

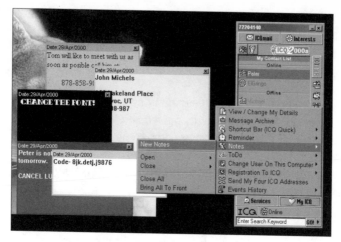

Figure 4.8 Notes all over my desktop.

▶ **Hide**—Close the note.

▶ **Always on Top**—Make the note always appear on top of any other window on your screen.

▶ **New**—Create a new note.

▶ **Delete Note**—Erase the note.

▶ **Text**—Choose to Cut, Copy, Paste, Delete, or Select All. This feature behaves in the same manner as similar features in a text editor or word processing program.

▶ **Appearance**—Change the way your note looks. Customize the fonts, font color, and background color.

▶ **Print As Text**—Print this note on regular paper.

▶ **File**—Import a text file or Export (Save) this note as a text file.

▶ **Add To Reminder**—Create a Reminder out of the note. You have to select how you want to trigger this reminder (refer to **Question 67** for details).

▶ **Send To Someone**—Send as a message to any, some, or all of your contacts.

▶ **Snap To Content**—Make the note window an appropriate size for the contents of the note.

▶ **Bring All To Top**—Cause all of your notes to always appear on top of other windows.

The more you use this ICQ feature and make it part of your life, the more you will appreciate its power. So often, when on the phone, we jot down a message on scrap paper that eventually gets thrown away, lost, or buried at the bottom of the pile. This feature solves all of those problems and truly helps you to organize part of your life.

 **I could be better at task management. Is there a way to organize my daily tasks into a to-do list?**

ICQ has a feature called **ToDo Notes** that works like a note and a reminder at the same time. It will remind you that you have to do things. It doesn't pop up like a reminder, but rather it stays on your screen as a note. You can find your ToDo notes by clicking the small 2do icon in the tray next to your ICQ flower (see **Figure 4.9**).

Figure 4.9 The ToDo Note and the 2do icon.

To create a new ToDo Note:

1. Click **My ICQ** button on your ICQ window.

2. Select **ToDo.**

3. Click **New.** This opens the **Add ToDo Event** window, which is very similar to the Add Reminder window, in which you can write a new ToDo Note or choose a preset ToDo Note by clicking Select Preset ToDo Note.

4. When you have finished writing your ToDo Note, click the **Add ToDo** button.

5 The 2do icon appears next to your ICQ flower in your icon tray. This icon gives you instant access to your ToDo List or a ToDo Note. Right-clicking the icon causes the following menu of options to appear:

▶ **New**—Opens the Add ToDo Event window, where you can write a new ToDo Note.

▶ **Open**—Shows you a list of all of your ToDo Notes. Clicking the name of the ToDo Note opens a History Event: Message window; the message inside this window is the ToDo Note.

▶ **Open ToDo List**—Launches the ICQ Message Archive on the ToDo section of the window.

ICQ E-Mail

Some tools are so useful that they persist despite other advances in technology. The telephone is a great real-world example. On the Internet, that technology is e-mail. Sending messages through e-mail is so much a part of the Internet that you can be assured that everyone connected to the Internet can send and receive e-mail. This isn't true of instant messaging today, but we predict it won't be long until instant messaging is just as ubiquitous as e-mail. In the meantime, ICQ has many excellent features that let you use e-mail as an integrated part of your ICQ-based communication strategy.

I am new on the Internet and need a good e-mail program. Can I use ICQ to send and receive e-mail?

ICQ has a built-in e-mail client that lets you check your e-mail and send e-mail messages. The advantage of using ICQ to check your e-mail is that it limits the number of programs you must have running on your desktop at one time. The ICQ Email Client program is pretty basic, and we don't recommend using it as your exclusive e-mail program. One of the big disadvantages is that the ICQ e-mail program doesn't really handle attachments, the files that people attach to e-mail messages. Another big disadvantage is that you will not be able to read e-mail messages longer than ninety-nine lines.

The best thing to do is to use ICQ as an e-mail preview. Let ICQ check your e-mail while you're online. You can respond to some of the short e-mail messages without launching your main e-mail program. When you do receive an e-mail that contains an attachment or that is longer than ninety-nine lines, you can launch your primary e-mail program and retrieve this e-mail from your e-mail server.

To configure ICQ as your e-mail client:

1. Click the **ICQ** button on your ICQ window.

2. Select **Preferences.**

3. From the menu select **Email.**

4. On the **Send Email Option** tab, choose the radio button labeled **Use ICQ Email Client** in the section labeled **Select the default ICQ Email Client.**

5. In the bottom part of this tab, enter the name of your SMTP server. If you don't know the name of your outgoing e-mail server, click the **SMTP Setup Help** button. ICQ will help you to determine the name of your SMTP server. This button opens your browser and takes you to the related ICQ help section.

6. Once your SMTP information is set up, click the **Email Alerts** tab.

7. Click the **Add** button. Now you can fill in the blanks on the other side of the window:

▶ **Description**—Type the name you want to call this account.

▶ **Mailbox Type**—ICQ currently works with POP3 servers and ICQ Mail. Use the ICQ Mail type only if you have an ICQ Web base e-mail address.

▶ **Mail Server**—This is the server that manages your e-mail. If you don't know your mail server, contact your Internet service provider.

▶ **Username**—The name you use to get your e-mail on the server.

▶ **Password**-The password your mail server expects.

Now you will be able to receive your e-mail messages through the ICQ Email Client.

The Email tabs

Lets take a look at some of the e-mail options that ICQ gives you through the Email tabs:

▶ **Notifications**—Check the box for ICQ to play a wave file when you receive new mail. Select the wave file by clicking on the Browse button.

▶ **Email Alerts**—Add the accounts you want ICQ to check for new email.

▶ **VIP**—Enter your friend's ICQ number or e-mail address so you will have them in your VIP list. When you have someone in your VIP list, ICQ will let you know when you get a message from that person. You will be notified that you have VIP mail.

▶ **Send Email Options**—Configure this tab to send e-mail using your ICQ mail client.

▶ **ICQmail Message**—If you are using an ICQ e-mail account, with this option you will be notified when you recieve an e-mail in that account. Select the wave file you want to play by checking the box and selecting a wave file from your computer.

▶ **ICQ Message**—Same as the above except this option is for regular e-mail (for all e-mail accounts you configure ICQ to check for new mail).

▶ **Check Email**—Configure the Check Email options, such as how often ICQ should check for new e-mail, from 1 to every 99 minutes. The launch options set when you would like the Email client started, for example, when you launch ICQ at startup. The Display Option: Display Email notification on Contact List if Email is assigned to user will alert you when someone in your contact list sends you an e-mail message using an ICQ email account.

Certainly, you have people who send you e-mail that you pay particular attention to. Make them a VIP and set up special notification when their e-mail arrives. Select the **VIP tab** to specify the name and e-mail address of your VIPs. Simply type their name and e-mail address and click the **Add** button in the VIP tab.

I already have an e-mail program. Should I still use ICQ to check my e-mail?

The ICQ Email Client is most effective when it is used with another e-mail client program, such as Outlook, Eudora, or one of the other popular e-mail programs. ICQ Email Client is a very simple and basic program. It does not have many of the features you may need when sending and receiving e-mail. For those functions, you should rely on a full-featured e-mail program.

Use the ICQ Email Client to check your e-mail. This way, you can check your e-mail whenever you want without loading your e-mail program. ICQ Email Client has basic e-mail capabilities, such as message preview and notification of an attachment.

CAUTION

The ICQ Email Client program works a little differently from other e-mail client programs. Erasing e-mail messages you receive in the ICQ Email Client program causes them to be erased from the e-mail server. This is bad if you are also using a full-featured e-mail client, as we've recommended. Once a message has been erased from the server, no other programs can retrieve it. Your message, once erased, will be permanently lost. Only erase messages in the ICQ Email Client after you have also received them in your primary e-mail client.

Using a single resource for many of your desktop tasks has its advantages. The Email Client program is just another of the many utilities presented by ICQ. You may find some or all of them useful. If you want more detailed information about setting up your ICQ Email Client program, refer to **Question 70**.

I've changed Internet service providers. How do I make changes to ICQ so that it can handle my e-mail?

Occasionally, you may change Internet server providers (ISPs). This can happen when you move or upgrade your service. When you change your ISP, you most often change your e-mail address as well. To change ICQ to handle your new e-mail address, you can either add a new e-mail account to your ICQ and erase the old one, or simply edit the old account and enter the new information.

To create a new account:

1. Click **Preferences.** This will open the Owner Preferences window in the Email option.

2. From the **Email Alerts** tab, click the **Add** button. Select the Mailbox Type, POP3 or ICQ Mail. You will see a new mail account appear in the Mail Accounts list, with the name New Account (and a number).

3. Click **"Check Email" Setup.** This opens the **ICQ EEC—Email Preferences** window, with the **Accounts** tab on top.

4. Click the Add button. You will see a new mail account appear in the Mail Accounts list, with the name New Account (and a number).

5. By changing the **Description** in the right pane, the Mail Account name will also change. Add your new information: Mail Server, User Name, and Password.

6. You will see the names of all the accounts you have created on the left side of the window. By unchecking the box, that account will be disabled. The ICQ Email Client won't check for new mail on that account. If you decide that you no longer have a reason for maintaining an account that you don't use, erase it by clicking the account name and then clicking the Delete button. You will be asked whether you are sure you want to erase this account; click Yes, and the account will be erased.

Remember that if you change ISPs, you'll probably also have to change your outgoing e-mail server to enable you to send e-mail from your ICQ Email Client. From the Owner Preference window on the Email option tab, change the SMTP Server. Click Apply when you are done.

Q73 Can I get a new e-mail address from ICQ?

There was a time when your only option was to get your e-mail address from your ISP. But technology has changed and now you can get your e-mail service from other sites on the Internet. In fact, you can have as many e-mail addresses as you want. There are hundreds of places on the Internet to get free e-mail addresses. Not to be outdone by anyone, you can have your own free ICQ e-mail address. You must first be a registered ICQ user to apply for a free account.

Visit the ICQ Web site to apply for your free e-mail address: **www.icq.com/icqmail/signup.html**. Or, click the ICQ button in the left top corner of your Contact List and select **Register a New Account.**

Once there, enter your ICQ number and your ICQ password. ICQ will look up your account and then allow you to set up your new e-mail account by selecting three possible ICQ addresses. Your new e-mail address will be *your choice*@icqmail.com.

After you sign up and receive your new e-mail address, you can check your e-mail from any Web browser by going to **www.icq.com/icqmail**.

Additionally, your ICQ program will alert you to incoming e-mail by flashing a new-mail icon. Double-click the icon to view your mail. You can also maintain an address list on the ICQ e-mail Web site. You can choose to e-mail people in your online Contact List or use the Web-based ICQ communications features to send the contact a message, page them, or chat with them.

Phone Center

As exciting as the Internet can be sometimes, it still hasn't replaced the good-old telephone. ICQ has made it much easier to contact people by phone, by providing the ability to look up your contact's current phone number.

Q74   What are some of the phone features of ICQ?

One of the most important features of ICQ as an instant messenger is that it enables you to know when people are available to contact. Simply checking your Contact List to see when people are online gives you an incredible amount of information. If your friend has a single phone line that she uses to connect to the Internet, and you see her online, you know it's a bad time to call on the phone. But, if she's online, and has a second modem line or cable modem to connect to the Internet, you know the chances are good that she'll be in to take your phone call. You can even send a special ICQ Phone Request message that says, "How come I am getting voice mail when I know you're there?" People can't hide behind their voice mail any longer.

Along the same lines, people are not always at the same phone number. Tracking down your friends so that you can call them is made easier with the **ICQ Phone-Follow Me** feature, discussed in detail in **Question 75**. Phone-Follow Me works for you, as well; let others know exactly how you can be reached with this feature. You can set your phone status just as you can set your ICQ status.

For people who still use the telephone for the bulk of their communications, ICQ can keep you from wearing out your dialing finger. **Question 78** tells you how to use the built-in ICQ phone dialer. Each of your contacts who gives you their phone number can be dialed, making ICQ a great way to keep your phone directory.

Keep up on the latest telephone features and how they are integrated into ICQ by visiting the ICQ Internet Telephony Network at **http://www.icq.com/telephony/telephony.html.** You can find other ICQ users with the same interests in telephony, join telephony-related lists, or create new lists on this ICQ Web page.

Lastly, ICQ has implemented a pay telephony service based on the Net2Phone network. Call any telephone in the world right from your PC. With the hardware necessary to use some of the basic voice features of ICQ, such as a microphone, speakers, and a sound card, you can use your PC like a telephone. Place your calls through your PC and dial a telephone. The person taking your call won't even know you are using a computer. The Net2Phone service is available from many places, but using the service through ICQ helps support future ICQ development.

What does it mean to have my phone number follow me?

Phone-Follow Me in ICQ should not be confused with an automated feature offered by some telephone companies called Follow Me. In ICQ, the Phone-Follow Me feature allows you to enter a telephone number for each of your possible locations. Then, as you move around during the day, you can update your location in ICQ. People who want to contact you by phone can look up your current location and corresponding phone number.

The Follow Me feature provided by some phone companies is similar. You provide the phone company with a list of phone numbers where you might be reached, and people calling your primary phone number are automatically call-forwarded to each number in the list until you are reached. The ICQ service requires you to update ICQ with your current location, but then people trying to reach you get you right away.

One of the best ways to store phone numbers is in your personal contact information. You can add a phone number for each of your possible locations. For example, your home, your cell phone, your office, your car, your gym, and so on.

To add telephone numbers for places where you can be reached:

1. Click the **ICQ** button in the ICQ window.

2. Click **View/Change My Details.**

3. Select the **Phone—Follow Me** tab.

4. Click the **Add** button to add a telephone number for a new location. You can give your location meaningful names, such as Home, Office, Club, Mobile, and so on.

After you add phone numbers to the Phone-Follow Me system, it's up to you to keep it up to date with your current location. Switching locations is simple. Follow the first three steps in the preceding list, then select your current location by clicking on the phone number where you are located. Then, click the **Set Current Location # button.**

 **How can I choose who sees my phone number?**

It's natural to be a little careful about giving your phone number out to just anyone on the Internet. This is particularly true when you've published personal information about yourself. On the other hand, you may want to make your number available to friends on your Contact List or to everyone for business purposes. ICQ gives you four options for deciding who gets to see your phone number:

▶ **Set ICQ to display response dialog**—The most secure way of publishing your number. Each time someone wants your number, they have to ask your permission to receive it.

▶ **Set ICQ to automatically accept**—Allows everyone to access your phone number automatically, without your knowledge.

▶ **Set ICQ to automatically decline**—No one gets your number.

▶ **Set ICQ to automatically decline from users that are not on my Contact List**—Limits the number of people who can have access to your number to only the people who are on your Contact List.

Here is how you can set this option:

1. Click the **ICQ** button on your ICQ window.
2. Select **Preferences.** The Owner Preference window will open.
3. Click the **Phone—Follow Me** option from the menu.
4. In the **Phone Authorization** tab you will find the above options.

How can I find my friend's most recent phone number?

One of the interesting things about the Phone-Follow Me feature is that to access someone's current phone number, they must be online. Unless they have a cellular modem or connect from multiple computers, it seems that if the user is online, you know where they are anyway.

To add phone numbers:

1. Click the contact's nickname in the **Contact List.**
2. Select **Phone-Follow Me** from the menu.
3. Select **Find Phone# and Dial** from the submenu.

Your contact's Phone-Follow Me Phone Book/Dialer will launch, listing each of the phone numbers and locations. You can see the Last Phone Location and the number to dial listed in the bottom of this window.

If you have a phone number for your contact that is not in the list (perhaps you have the cellular number that is not given out to others), you can add this number to the list that appears in the **Phone Book/Dialer** window. Click the Add button, and the **User Details** window will launch in the **Phone-Follow Me** tab. Notice in this window that you can also click the button that will update the phone numbers whenever the user is online.

Can I dial a phone number using ICQ?

ICQ has the ability to dial a phone number for you by playing Dial Tone Modulation Frequency (DTMF) tones through your computer's speakers. DTMF tones are the semimusical tones you hear when you dial the telephone. Your telephone creates these tones, which vary in pitch, based on the number you dial. Any device that can make those sounds has the ability to dial your phone.

When your contacts have entered their telephone numbers and given you access to them, you can use ICQ as a dialer to telephone them. To use ICQ to dial a phone number, follow these steps:

1. Click the contact's nickname to open the menu.

2. Select **Phone-Follow Me** from the menu.

3. Select **Find Phone# and Dial.**

4. When the Phone-Follow Me window launches, select the phone number from the list of phone numbers that appears. Your contact may have only a single phone number entered.

5. Lift your telephone handset and make sure you have a dial tone.

6. Hold the telephone handset up to your computer's speakers so that the mouthpiece is close to the speaker. (Make sure that your computer speaker volume is set moderately high.)

7. In the Phone-Follow Me window, click the **Click to Dial** button.

ICQ will play the DTMF tones through your computer's speakers and into your telephone handset, thus dialing the number. If holding the telephone handset up to the speakers while you dial is not a problem for you, this feature will be useful for you.

Can I get messages on my cell phone via ICQ?

The world has turned to the abbreviated message. On the nightly news, these short messages are called sound bites. In ICQ, they're called instant messages, and on cell phones, they're called short messages. So far, we've covered how ICQ has integrated with other programs over the Internet, with the Web and its information systems, and with the legacy telephone. It's now possible to use the services of ICQ to send short messages to almost any cellular phone in the world, for free.

Digital cell phones equipped with Short Message Service (SMS) can receive small text-only messages from the Internet. Short messages are less than 160 characters long. Many digital phones that support the GSM standard offer SMS service.

A leader in digital messaging, ICQ didn't want to be left out of this mobile telecommunications messaging technology. ICQ provides a registry for its users. By registering on the ICQ SMS site, at **www.icq.com/sms/**, you can allow other ICQ users and visitors to the ICQ Web site to find your SMS number and send you a short message. Register here, or find others around the world who might like to get a short message from you.

Please keep in mind that, like ICQ, users of SMS also want you to respect their privacy. Please do not use the ICQ SMS registry to market your products or services. The Short Message Service is a valuable tool that should not become filled with spam.

Integrating ICQ with Telephony and Games

By now, you may think that ICQ has just about every type of utility built into it. However, as many wonderful features as ICQ has, it doesn't have everything. What is great about ICQ is that it can serve as the central control panel for just about everything. There are many telephone programs and games that can be closely integrated with the ICQ program.

I want to video conference—can ICQ help me?

No video conferencing capability is built into ICQ. But ICQ has been designed so that you can use one of the other popular video conferencing programs that are tightly integrated with the ICQ program. Microsoft NetMeeting is a popular collaboration program that gives you video conferencing capability along with application sharing, a whiteboard, and a limited chat. It's by no means the only software program that works with ICQ, however.

Click one of the contacts in your Contact List to bring up the menu, and then select **Internet Telephony/Games.** Select **Other** from this menu, and you will see which external communications applications you currently have installed on your computer. To see the other possible applications, select **View List—Download** from this menu, and you will see a display of software.

Selecting one of the software packages from this list of supported software causes ICQ to attempt to launch the software program. If it's not installed on your computer, you will be prompted to go to the product homepage to download and install the product. The product **CU-SeeMe,** for example, provides great color video conferencing. A commercial version is available from White Pines, and a free version is available from Cornell University. If you'd like to download the free version of CU-SeeMe, don't click the ICQ Go to Product Home Page button. Instead, point your Web browser to **www.rocketcharged.com/cu-seeme/download.html**.

This site has links to commercial and free versions for many different operating systems. Download and install CU-SeeMe or some other video conferencing software, and you will see it listed as an external application that can be started right from ICQ rather than from your Windows Start menu.

The size of the video conference window that appears depends on the video conferencing software and the ability of your video camera. **Figure 4.10** shows a small video window using Microsoft NetMeeting.

Figure 4.10 Video conference with your contacts by using NetMeeting.

Not only can you use ICQ to launch an external application, you can also send requests to your contacts to communicate using one of these external programs. To send a request, follow the next steps:

1. Click your contact's nickname.

2. From the menu, select **Internet Telephony/Games** and then select **Other.**

3. From the list of installed applications that appears, choose one by clicking it.

4. When the **Phone/Video/Data Request** window launches, enter a subject or message for your session.

Your request will be sent to your contact. They can either accept your request, launching the application required to communicate, or send you a message back letting you know that they do not have the software installed. Normally, you must both have the same software application installed on your computers to be able to communicate. Once the request has been accepted, the program will start, and you can both begin communicating with this external software. Remember that ICQ has many features not installed in other software, such as file transfer, that you can use while using other software programs.

Q81 I just installed NetMeeting, but ICQ doesn't see it; what can I do?

ICQ does a good job of finding applications you have installed on your computer, but it's not flawless. Programs such as NetMeeting, Microsoft Chat, Vocaltec Iphone, and others are called *external applications* because they are external to ICQ. Sometimes, you just have to help ICQ locate the place on your hard drive where an external application has been installed. First, you must know where the external application is installed. If you are not sure, you can use Windows Explorer to locate the software program, by using the Find tool.

Once you know where your new external program (such as NetMeeting) is installed, follow these steps to set the location in ICQ:

1. Click the **ICQ button** on the ICQ window.

2. Select **Preferences**.

3. In the Owner Preferences window that lauches, select the **Telephony/Data/Games** menu.

4. Look for the external application that you installed in the list that appears on this window. When you find it, select it, and click the **Edit** button to the right.

5. The name of the external application appears. You may change it or leave it the way it is by default. Most importantly, you must then include a path to the executable program that runs your external application. (This normally has either an .exe or .com file extension.)

6. Use the **Browse** button to simplify entering the path. Locate the executable file on your hard drive and select it.

Some applications also require certain command-line parameters, which is the information the program needs when it first starts. This requirement is now fairly unusual. If your program has startup parameters, refer to the user guide for your product.

Your external application will now appear in the list with a small icon next to it, and it will be set up so that you can launch it from ICQ and send requests to other users to communicate using that program.

ICQ has a list of programs to download. Are these the only programs that work with ICQ?

ICQ has a list of some popular communications and game programs. You aren't limited to using only these programs. If you find a game or communications program that will work over the Internet, then by all means install it and use it with ICQ. The external program feature of ICQ can launch any type of program.

If you have an external program that you'd like to use that was not in the list, follow these steps:

1. Install the application you want to use with ICQ, being careful to remember where the application is installed on your hard drive. You need that information in Step 6.

2. Click the **ICQ button** on the ICQ window.

3. Select **Preferences.**

4. In the Owner Preferences window that launches, select the **Internet Telephony/Data/Games** menu.

5. Click the **New External** button.

6. Enter the name of the application you have installed.

7. Enter the path to the application's executable program. You can use the **Browser** button to make this simpler.

8. Click the **Update List** button.

Your application will now be available whenever you click a contact's name and select the Internet Telephony/Games menu choice. You can now find programs that have features not installed by ICQ and still use all the great features of ICQ.

Q83 With so many programs, how do I know which ones work best for me?

The most important consideration when using network software to collaborate with your contacts is that you and your contacts have the same software. For example, if you'd like to video conference using NetMeeting, and your friends all have CU-SeeMe, all you'll see is the Microsoft logo staring back at you. You should install CU-SeeMe if that's the program your friends are using.

Another consideration in choosing which programs to install has to do with the type of computer you are using. If you are using a Macintosh and select software that will only run on a Macintosh, the chances that you will be able to collaborate with someone using a PC are very slim.

Make certain that the software you are considering will work with your computer hardware. Verify from the installation information that you:

▶ Have enough memory

▶ Are running the right version of the operating system

▶ Have any extra hardware you might need, such as a CD-ROM drive, camera, or joystick controller

▶ Have a large enough hard drive

▶ Have a version of the software that is compatible with your contact's version

Of course, when you install programs that require all types of hardware, the person you are going to communicate with needs the same types of hardware. Be kind to your friends and don't select the most expensive software and hardware configurations unless you know they can all afford it.

Q84   I want to find someone to play a game with online. Where do I look?

Sometimes, the ICQ program can seem like a big game. But, alas, ICQ has no games to play. Game players use ICQ as a way to communicate with each other while playing games over the Internet and as a shortcut to games installed on their computers.

The ICQ Game Center

The ICQ Game Center can help you find other people who want to play games, learn more about configuring ICQ for gaming, and get technical support. You can find the ICQ Game Center at **www.icq.com/icqtour/games.html**.

There are many ways to find people on the Internet with whom to play games. ICQ has some Web utilities that make it easier. The **ICQ Game Request** is a Web-based utility that enables you to see what games are being played, see how many people are playing them, and request a game with others. You can find the ICQ Game Request at **www.icq.com/gamerequest/**.

When you load the **Game Request Web** page, you're provided with some information about Game Requests, and you're given a menu along the left side of the page. Click the **Now Playing** button on the Game Request Web page to view a list of games and the number of people playing them. Clicking the **View** button in the list of games that appears will present you with more information on the players, options for communicating with the players, and a link to add yourself to the game.

Another place to find people interested in playing games with you is through the ICQ Games Network at **www.icq.com/networks/Games/**.

The ICQ Games Network page lists every type of game you can conceive of (except Chutes and Ladders). Find the game you are interested in playing and then click it to search the ICQ directory for other ICQ users. You can search chat rooms, message boards, personal white pages, chat requests, and more. After you find people whom you'd like to play with, you can contact them using ICQ and ask them to play with you.

Another place to get information on playing games with other ICQ users is by searching the ICQ **ActiveLists** for information on games as shown in **Figure 4.11**. (**Section 5** has detailed information on using and creating ICQ ActiveLists.) ActiveLists are communities of ICQ users formed around common interests. Some of those interests include games. When you search for ActiveLists based on a topic, you can select Games as the topic. You can then choose a subtopic to further narrow your search. These are the four Games subtopics:

► Board Games

► Computer Games

► Console Games

► Social Games

Figure 4.11 Find communities of gamers using ICQ ActiveLists.

The original Internet communities—in some ways the precursor to ActiveLists—are the Usenet newsgroups. If you have access to Usenet News, and have a news reader installed, you can post messages and read messages posted by other multiplayer gamesters:

1. From your **Usenet News reader,** access the news server at ICQ: **news.icq.com**.

2. Select the newsgroup alt.games.multiplayer.ICQ.

3. A list of messages from this newsgroup will load into your news reader software. Using your news reader software, you can also post messages that will be read by others interested in multiplayer games.

The Impressive Web Search

When it comes to finding information, the Web has replaced the home encyclopedia. Those old books look great on bookshelves, but when it comes to finding out the tour dates of your favorite band, volumes 1 through 26 just don't cut it. Once again, ICQ is a tool that has it all. Find that Web information fast with ICQ.

I am looking for information on the Web. Can ICQ help me?

Finding information on the Internet using ICQ is simple. Right on the front of the ICQ window is a textbox in which you can enter your search word or words (see **Figure 4.12**). That's where the fun begins. Clicking the small arrow button next to the Web Search text box launches a menu from which you can choose any of twelve different types of searches (see **Table 4.1**). For example, if you are trying to locate a friend, you might choose to search using the **Web and People Search.**

Table 4.1—Web Search Selections

Selection	Description
Web and People Search	Search Using the ICQiT Web Search Engine.
Most Popular Web Results	Do a search through ICQ's most popular results of searches through the Web, ICQ lists, the ICQ site, and ICQ Groups. View related searches.
ICQ.com Communities	Search all or portions of the ICQ Web site for your keyword(s).
Web Search Engines	Search through any of the seventeen top Internet search engines listed in this menu selection.
Usenet Discussion Groups	Do a search through the Usenet newsgroups using one of the popular Web-based Usenet sites.
Software/Files	Looking for software to download? Search some of the best software download sites.
Reference	Use when you need to look up a word or a synonym.
Translation	Translate many of the world's languages to and from English.
News Articles	Search through World, Finance, Sports, and Technology news.
Stock Quotes	Query the stock market using one of the three services available.
Weather	Get the weather anywhere in the U.S.
Miscellaneous	Do a domain name search through Network Solutions; search for people using Whowhere; and find movie titles using the Internet Movie Database.

Figure 4.12 Hiding out in the open is the powerful ICQ Web Search.

Type your query in the text box and select the type of search, and your query is sent out over the Web. Of course, that means you need to be connected to the Internet when you do your searches. Also, if you are doing the same type of query multiple times, you can simply type your query term and click the small Go button next to the text box.

TIP

If the Web Search does not appear on your ICQ window, you might have to adjust your preferences. Launch the Preferences window and select the Contact List tab. Make certain that the selection labeled Remove Contact List Buttons is not selected. When this preference is checked, some of the features that normally appear on the ICQ window will not appear. The Web Search is one of those features.

Search engines and information resources have put much of the world's information online. Sifting through it to find your specific query is not always easy. Be patient. Try different search engines and change your query to be more specific if the results you get back don't seem to be meeting your needs. The **ICQ Web Search** is one of the Internet's better one-stop resources for finding information.

An example of using the Web Search might be to plan your vacation. Honolulu is one of the loveliest places on the planet. Not unlike many of the other lovely places on the planet, it has its good-weather days and bad-weather days. Using the ICQ Web Search, you can check the weather anywhere in the United States. Unfortunately, this service has not been expanded to include international weather yet.

Type the name of the city and state, separated by a comma, in the ICQ Web Search text box. Click the small arrow button next to the text box to launch the menu. Select Weather and one of the weather services from the menu. A Web page will launch and provide you with the requested weather.

Me Inglish not is good. Are there translators to help me?

The Internet, once an English-only phenomenon, is slowly waking up to the rest of the multilingual world. ICQ has many foreign-language features that will help you adapt it to your primary language. Make sure you visit the ICQ Language Center at **www.icq.com/languages/**.

Section 3 of this book, "Customizing ICQ," discusses some of the ways you can customize ICQ to "speak your language" by installing a foreign-language sound scheme. But none of these things will help you when you're in Poughkeepsie and trying to chat with someone in Brazil. If Portuguese just isn't on the list of languages you speak, you can use some of the Internet translation utilities. ICQ has a translator that is closely integrated with a couple different Web services—Babylon and AltaVista.

To use the Babylon or AltaVista translator, make sure you are connected to the Internet. These translation services are Web pages that receive information from your ICQ program. Type your word or phrase in the **ICQ Web Search text box** on the ICQ window. Then, click the small right-arrow button next to the Web Search text box and select **Translation** from the menu. You are presented with the Babylon services first in the menu, and the AltaVista services second. Your Web browser will launch and your translation will appear in the Web page.

TIP

The AltaVista service is better at translating short phrases than the Babylon service. You can also translate from other languages into English.

After you select a translation service, type a phrase in the ICQ Web Search text box and click the **Go** button to automatically use the same service to translate the new word or phrase. If you select the AltaVista service, you can ask this service to translate fairly large text documents by cutting and pasting them into the AltaVista translation text box. Buena Suerte!

Section 5
ICQ Communities

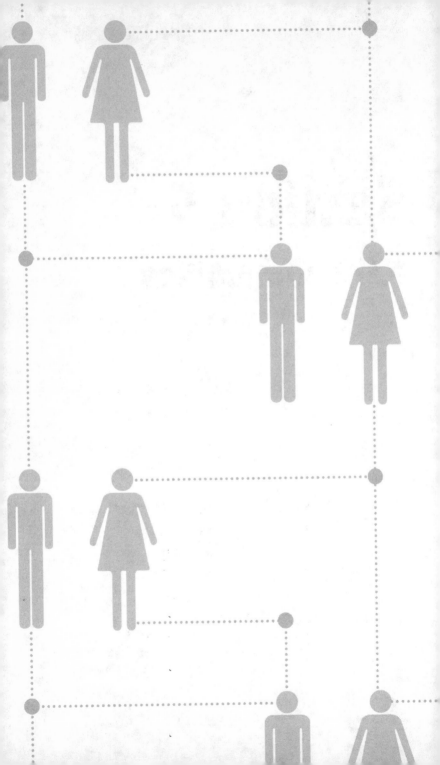

ICQ Communities

Making New Friends

Q87

I am bored and want to find someone to chat with. Can I use ICQ to find someone who wants to chat with a stranger?

It's so easy to make new friends using ICQ. You'll be surprised how many new and different kinds of friends you can make over the Internet by using ICQ. Besides Chat with a Friend (refer to **Question 27**), ICQ has other ways for you to find a chat partner or groups of people who are interested in chatting with people sharing similar interests.

Just about everyone has heard of chat rooms. Along with e-mail, they are almost synonymous with the Internet and are a favorite pastime of millions of people. ICQ has become one of the most popular ways to chat, partly because it's so easy. ICQ has made it very easy for users to create their own *chat rooms,* places where strangers gather to chat and become friends.

Chat rooms are operated and run by the owner/creator of the ICQ chat. Chat rooms are given their own ICQ numbers and can appear in your Contact List the same as any other contact. Once you add a chat room to your Contact List, you can send messages, URLs, files, and, of course, chat. The owner of the chat room connects all of his or her online contacts who want to chat into a single session so that everybody can join in.

You are just about guaranteed to find a chat room that interests you. Countless chat rooms can be found on every imaginable topic. New ones are created every day. You can visit the ICQ Web pages to find the chat that interests you. When you find one, simply add it to your Contact List. There are two ways to add a chat room to your Contact List:

If you have the ICQ chat number, just add it like a regular user:

1. Click the **ICQ button** in the ICQ window.
2. Select **Add/Invite User.**
3. Click **Find User—Add to the List.**
4. Enter the ICQ chat number in the third option and click Next.
5. Select the name of the chat room and click Next.

The chat room should appear in your Contact List, unless you need to be authorized. In that case, ask for authorization and wait until the owner of the chat room answers.

The other way to add a chat is from the Web. Open a Web browser and go to **www.icq.com/icqchat**. Select from the list of groups that share your interest. Select again from a more specific list, narrowing your search. You will now see the list of chat rooms that are available (online) at that moment. To add them to your **Contact List,** click the **Add Room to Contact List** button. Most of the time, this button displays either a green or white flower.

Occasionally, chat rooms require authorization from the owner. In this case, a small dialog box will appear requesting your reason for joining. Enter your reason and click **Request.** You will be notified when your request is answered.

Once the chat room is in your Contact List and the chat room is online, request a chat session. If other members of the chat are connected, you will be able to chat with them. We recommend using the IRC-style Chat mode in these types of chats. The IRC style makes it much easier to read and follow the conversations.

 **Are there Web-based ICQ chat rooms that I can join?**

Originally, ICQ was a simple program for messaging and chat. As ICQ has grown and matured into a multifaceted communications program, it has become very integrated into other Internet technologies, such as the World Wide Web. The ICQ programmers have created a Web component that can be embedded into Web pages that allows you to chat using the ICQ IRC client, called IrCQ.

The IrCQ-Net works almost exactly the same way as the traditional Internet Relay Chat (IRC). The major difference between IRC and IrCQ is that the IrCQ-Net is Java-based so that it runs in a Web page. The IrCQ also has additional features, such as the capability to add your ICQ number and e-mail address to your information for other people to see. Another cool feature is that you can reserve your nickname, which means that only you can use that nickname on the IrCQ network.

Like IRC, on IrCQ-Net you can communicate with people all around the world. You can join a public chat room or create your own private chat room. Have as many chat windows open at the same time as you want.

To see IrCQ commands go to **www.icq.com/ircqnet/help/#how**.

Q89   Can I start my own chat room?

After you've participated in other people's chat rooms, you'll soon want to start one of your own. You can start your own chat room by using the ICQ Chat Rooms feature or the IrCQ-Net.

Begin creating your chat room using the ICQ Chat Rooms feature by registering a new ICQ number:

1. Click the **My ICQ** button on your ICQ window.

2. Select **Registration To ICQ** from the menu.

3. Click **Register a New User.**

4. Use the **Registration to ICQ** (as explained in **Question 5**) to complete your registration.

To register as a chat room instead of as a normal user with a nickname, type the name of the chat room in place of the nickname, but use the & symbol before the name of the chat room (see **Figure 5.1**). This symbol will help other users identify you as a chat room. Instead of typing your first name, type the category name in which you want your ICQ chat room to be identified.

To see the list of categories available in ICQ, go to **www.icq.com/icqchat/index.html**. Add as much information as you want about your chat room. It's important that you add some information about your chat room, such as what the chat is all about and what kind of people should join. With sufficient information, people can decide whether or not to join your chat room, and it's easier for other members to find your chat using a search.

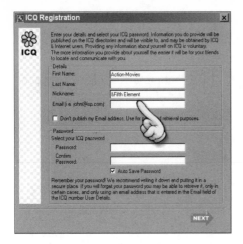

Figure 5.1 Adding the & symbol identifies this ICQ number as a chat room.

Your chat room will be publicized on the **ICQ Newly Created ICQ Chats Web page** within twelve hours after you register. People will be able to add your chat room to their list immediately from this page.

Your chat room will be open for business as soon as you go online with the ICQ network. Running a chat room makes you the *ChatMaster,* who has complete control of his or her chat rooms. The ChatMaster decides who can participate in a chat session and who can be kicked out and even can deny entry to their chats. Being a ChatMaster is fun and, in a way, ChatMasters have their own community.

The ICQ chat room will be open as long as you are online. When you go offline, your chat room will be closed and no new members will be able to join. If members are still chatting when you go offline, the chat server will continue running the session until all the members have left.

Your chat will be visible in the ICQ Chat directories as long as you keep the category information in the First Name field of the chat's user details. If you get too many members and no longer want to advertise your group in the ICQ Chat directories, simply erase the category information from the First Name field.

Does ICQ have other ways for me to make friends?

ICQ has various meeting places that are accessible to everyone. **Table 5.1** lists the names of some of these meeting places, a short description of each, and its URL.

Table 5.1—Meeting Places on ICQ

Name	Description	Where to Find It
ICQ List	List of ICQ users who share the same interest.	**www.icq.com/icqlist/**
ICQ Groups	Lists of people grouped by similar interests; different from the ICQ List because they operate differently.	**http://groups.icq.com**
ICQ Chat Rooms	Created by ICQ users. Learn more about Chat Rooms in **Question 87** and **Question 89**.	**www.icq.com/icqchat/**
ICQ Virtual Communities	The ICQ List and ICQ Groups can form the foundation of a Virtual Community. Members of of the Virtual Community are normally located in a single individual's Contact List.	**www.icq.com/ communities/cyber- communities.html**
ICQ Message Boards	A place where people can post and read messages, which can be single messages or entire topic threads.	**www.icq.com/boards/**
Game Request	Meet people who want to play a specific game. To understand how the Game Request works, see **Question 84**.	**www.icq.com/ gamerequest/**

Name	Description	Where to Find It
IrCQ-Net	The ICQ Java version of the popular Internet application, IRC. See **Question 88**.	**www.icq.com/ircqnet/**
CQ People Navigator	Has most of the meeting places organized by category. You must browse through categories and subcategories.	**www.icq.com/ people/topic.html**
ICQ Networks	Works almost exactly like the ICQ People Navigator. Using this feature, you can be more specific in your search for a meeting place.	**www.icq.com/ networks/**
ICQ People Rings	Groups of Web pages that share a single topic, interconnected by a special Web ring navigation bar.	**www.icq.com/icqring/**
ActiveLists	The easiest communities to access and interact with their members. Gives you direct access to the members right on your Contact List.	

Another cool way to meet new people, chat, and surf the Internet all at the same time is by installing the new ICQ plug-in called ICQ Surf. With the ICQ Surf tool, when you open a browser, ICQ lets you communicate with others visiting the same Web page. While viewing a Web page, you are shown the number of people visiting the page and are given the option to chat with them in a special Web chat that appears at the bottom of the Web page you are visiting.

You can download the ICQ Surf Alpha version using the ICQ FTP site at **ftp://ftp.icq.com/pub/ICQ_Win95_98_NT4/ICQ_Surf.exe**.

To download ICQ Surf:

1. Click the **Services** button on your ICQ **Contact List** window.

2. Select **ICQ Surf.** A new window will appear with a link to download ICQ Surf.

3. Select a folder where to store the downloaded file.

4. Once it has finished downloading, using Windows Explorer, go to the folder where you saved the ICQ Surf installation file and click it to begin the installation process.

To run ICQ Surf once it has been installed:

1. Click the **Services** button on your ICQ Contact List window.

2. Select ICQ Surf.

Customize ICQ Surf for your Web surfing needs. For more information on ICQ Surf, go to the ICQ Surf homepage at **www.icq.com/icqsurf**.

ICQ Directories

Some people choose to list themselves in the phone book, while others prefer to remain anonymous. ICQ gives you the same choice, by allowing you to either remain anonymous or publish your information in the ICQ directory.

Q91 Is it safe to put my name in ICQ directories?

In a word, no. Remember that any information you add in your ICQ personal details will be publicized on the Web, and anyone with a Web browser can check it out. If you wish to keep your personal information private, it's a good idea not to list any information in your details other than your nickname and your initials. The bad thing about not publishing information is that it will be difficult for long-lost friends to find you.

The ICQ White Pages directory is used mostly by other members of ICQ who are looking for either friends or people with similar interests. The ICQ White Pages search is impressive. It has a lot of options you can use in your search to make your search very thorough. An advantage of the ICQ directory in finding people with common interests is that you can choose to search only for people who are currently online. This way, you don't get old, unused ICQ addresses or people who never use their computers.

CAUTION

You should check to see what type of information your children are including in their personal user information. It may conflict with what you feel is safe to publish on the Internet.

There are no guarantees, but we've never heard of a case where someone has used information obtained from the ICQ directory to do bad things to anyone. Publishing your information is a matter of personal choice. The safest thing is to not publish your information. But, if you are using ICQ so that you can make new friends and hope that old friends and family will find you through ICQ, put as much information into the directory as you feel comfortable publishing in a public directory.

How can I put my information in the ICQ White Pages directory?

All the information that you provide ICQ when you register is entered automatically into the ICQ White Pages. The only information you can enter into your personal information that you have the option of not publishing in the ICQ White Pages is your primary e-mail address and password. If you choose not to publish them, they will not appear in the ICQ White Pages.

You can add or change information in the ICQ White Pages at any time after you've registered for the first time. If you are going to maintain information in the ICQ White Pages, it's a good idea to keep the information current.

To add or change information about yourself in the ICQ White Pages:

1. Click the **Services** button on your ICQ window.

2. Select **ICQ White Pages** from the menu.

3. Click **Publicize in White Pages**. The **ICQ Global Directory: My Details** window will open.

4. Go through the tabs and add or change all the information that you want other people to see about you.

5. When you've finished adding information, click **Save**.

6. To close the window, click **Done**.

The ICQ White Pages are instantly updated. People who search the ICQ White Pages will be able to see your information and contact you. Try doing some searches through the ICQ White Pages yourself to find out how simple it is to find people. Look for old school friends, past associates, or people who share your interests.

ActiveLists

ActiveLists are very similar to e-mail lists you can join on the Internet, where members of the list can broadcast messages to all the other members or choose to send e-mail to a single person in the group. ActiveLists work in much the same way, except instead of using e-mail, you broadcast ICQ messages. This is one way to keep your e-mail unclogged, and the real-time aspect makes communicating with ActiveList members much more interesting and fun. When you want to communicate privately with one or a few members, you can choose to communicate with them privately in a chat, through direct e-mail, or select specific contacts from your Contact List. That is much more control than you have using e-mail list servers.

How can I join a community of ICQ members who share my interest?

If your ICQ program is in Advanced mode and configured to display the ICQuick bar or Shortcut Bar on the ICQ Contact List window, you should then configure the ICQuick bar from the Owner Preferences window to include the ActiveList button. Clicking the ActiveList icon on the Contact List window will cause a thin button, labeled **Find/Add An ICQ ActiveList,** to appear. Clicking the button launches the **ICQ ActiveList Search Wizard.** The first two options, **Search by List ID**# and **Search by List Title Name** are useful if you already know which ActiveList you want to participate in.

The third option in the wizard, **Search by Category,** allows you to find lists by narrowing your search. Select this option by checking the check box and clicking the Next button. The next window in the wizard allows you to narrow your search by topic and language.

You will see a **Press to edit Topic/Keywords** button. Ignore the check box next to it. It's unimportant at this point. Clicking this button launches the **Selected Interests** window (see **Figure 5.2**). Select a topic from the window on the left, and a list of **Suggested Interests** will appear in the window on the right. Clicking any of the interests will cause it to expand into a list of specific interests. Look through this list of topics, and when you find the one that interests you the most, double-click it, (or single-click to highlight it) and then click the **Add** button. Both methods should add this topic into the list of Selected Interests on the far right. You can have a single selected interest to search on. When you have finished adding topics, click **OK**.

Figure 5.2 Select one or more topics to search for ActiveLists.

After you select your interest to search on, you are returned to the ActiveList Search Wizard, where you can next specify a language. This is useful for limiting your searches to a single spoken language, assuming that you aren't fluent in all the world's languages. You should select the language you are most comfortable reading and the one you believe might contain your particular interest. For example, selecting Surfing as an interest and Bosnian as a language might not get you the ActiveList you were hoping to join.

Click the Next button and a list of ActiveLists will be displayed. You can choose to join one or more lists. Highlight the list by clicking it, and then click the AddList button in the bottom of the window. If you are adding only a single list, you can highlight the list and click the Next button.

Some lists allow you to join automatically, and others require the approval of the owner of the list. The ActiveList is added to your Contact List, and once you have been added, the other members of the list will appear in the ActiveList section of your Contact List. To view these members, click the ICQ ActiveList button on the top of the ActiveList section.You can choose to hide your lists by clicking the Hide All button at the top of your ICQ window. After you become a member, you are free to send messages, request chats, and use all the other features available to a contact. You will not have to request their permission to add them as contacts.

Q94 Who runs the ActiveList?

When ICQ users install the ActiveList server software, described in **Question 95**, they are free to create and launch as many lists as they like. They are considered owners of any list they start. They can also host lists for which other people are administrators. The owner of the ActiveList can appoint others to be administrators. This is similar to the old days of the BBS (bulletin board system), where owners of the bulletin board would appoint others to be system operators (sysops for short). The owner of the list can delegate Admin authority to the other administrators but retains full control over the list. The owner can change the administrator's rights (see **Figure** 5.3), just as administrators can change member's rights.

Some of the abilities of administrators are the following:

▶ Broadcast Admin messages to the members of the list

▶ Create and delete chat rooms for the ActiveList

▶ Create and delete forums (message boards) as well as delete individual messages

▶ View the ActiveList server Log files

▶ Take the ActiveList server online and offline

▶ Change the server settings

▶ Remove, ban, disconnect, and edit member rights

Figure 5.3 List owners and administrators manage the ActiveList.

I can't find any ActiveLists about growing celery. Can I start my own ActiveList?

Celery growing may not be on the top of everyone's list to join, but that's what makes ActiveLists special. When you have a topic for which there is no current list, or there are current lists on that topic but you don't want to join them, you can create your own ActiveList. To run your own ActiveList, you must install the ActiveList server software.

First, download the free ActiveList server from the ICQ FTP site at **ftp://ftp.icq.com/pub/ICQ_Win95_98_NT4/Addons/ActiveList.exe.**

Here is some information you should know before you start installing the ActiveList server. First, the ActiveList server works only while it is connected to the Internet. You can run the ActiveList server from your PC, but if you have a dial-up connection to the Internet that does not stay connected all the time, members of your list will become discouraged by not having access to your list whenever they want it. It's better to find someone with a dedicated connection to the Internet to host your ActiveList server software.

Another consideration of where to host your ActiveList is the amount of bandwidth you have in your Internet connection. If you are connected over a 56.6 modem or slower, you probably don't want to host an ActiveList server. With a moderately sized list, your bandwidth can be consumed fairly quickly with people accessing the server.

After you download and install the server, you are ready to create a new ActiveList. One strange thing that you should know is that you must run a new ActiveList server for each ActiveList you want to host. You might have thought that running the ActiveList server allows you to host multiple lists, as with a Web server. This just isn't the case.

Start the **ICQ ActiveList** server from the **Start** menu. This starts the ActiveList administrator. Click the **Register** button, which launches the ICQ ActiveList Registration window. Select **Register a New ICQ ActiveList.** Click the **Next** button.

Enter your ICQ# and password, so that you become the owner. If you are not going to be the owner, type the ICQ# and password of the person who will be the owner of this ActiveList. Click **Next.** Continuing to the next window, set the list's subject. Click the **Edit** button to launch the **Selected Interests** window, like the one shown earlier in this section. **Select a topic** and click the **Add** button. Then click the **OK** button. Enter any member requirements in the text box on the ActiveList details window, and, finally, select any spoken languages this list might be limited to. Click **Next.**

You now have the opportunity to enter a lengthy, detailed description of your ActiveList. If you have many points, consider putting them in concise bullet points so that people don't have to read through tons of text. Click **Next**. (Yes, this is a very long process. Hang in there.) Next, you get to describe the connection of the machine that is hosting the ActiveList server. Select your connection type, LAN or modem. Don't change the other ICQ ActiveList port selection from its default, dynamic setting. We're getting near the end here. Click **Next**.

These are the security settings. You can choose to **Auto Accept** requests to join your list or require people to be authorized first. Choose whether your directory listing includes your online/offline status, and, finally, type a password for this list. Make it easy to remember. Test your memory by typing it again in the **Confirm Password** field. If your list is successfully registered, the next window lets you know you were successful. Click **Next** and, on the last window, click **Done**.

Start your ActiveList from the Start menu. You will see a window that shows you member information and online status and allows you to launch the **Admin Tool** and set preferences for the ActiveList (see **Figure 5.4**). Start the ActiveList server and specify which list you'd like to start.

Figure 5.4 The ActiveServer List window displays important online status and member information.

How do I invite people to join my ActiveList?

If you have an extensive Contact List, you might consider starting there to invite people to your ActiveList. Right-click the name of the ActiveList in your Contact List, and in the menu that pops up, click **ICQ ActiveList Invitation** button. When the ActiveList window launches, click the check box next to the ActiveList to which you want to invite people. It can be your ActiveList, or if you are authorized by another ActiveList, you can send out invitations to join that list as well. Select the recipients of your invitation by checking the box next to their nickname in the invitation window. Unfortunately, this may not allow you to send many invitations. You must find people interested in your list and invite them by sending an ICQ message, e-mail, or other type of message.

When sending messages to invite people to join your ActiveList, make sure you include the ICQ ActiveList number in your message, making it simple for them to join. To make it even easier, include directions for adding an ActiveList, similar to those given in **Question 93**. Instead of using the topic search, you will be providing them with the exact number of the list.

Do I always have to be connected to an ActiveList?

You can be connected all the time to ActiveLists or disconnected during certain times. It's up to you to choose when you're connected to the ActiveList. Also, you can be connected to as many ActiveLists as you want. You can choose to be connected to some ActiveLists and disconnected from others. Sometimes you'll be busy and prefer not to receive ActiveList messages. You can disconnect from the list and reconnect when you are ready. Messages will not be queued up. You will miss any ActiveList messages sent while you were disconnected from the ActiveList.

To disconnect from an ActiveList:

1. From your ICQ window, right-click the **ActiveList name.**

2. From the menu that appears, click **Disconnect.**

You will be disconnected only from that ActiveList. If you have more ActiveLists from which you want to disconnect, repeat the preceding two steps.

If you have already joined an ActiveList, you may have noticed that every time you connect, the ActiveList is automatically connected. This feature is nice when you belong to only one ActiveList, especially one with relatively few members. If you belong to three or four ActiveLists with many members, however, it will take a long time for your ICQ to load. When you belong to multiple lists, it's a good idea to have the autoconnect feature disabled and then connect manually to the ActiveList in which you want to participate.

To disable the autoconnect feature, you have to follow these steps for each ActiveList you have joined:

1. Right-click the **ActiveList name** in your ICQ window.

2. From the menu, uncheck the option called **Connect At Startup** by clicking it once.

On the left side of each ActiveList name is a little ball icon. These icons show the status of the ActiveList. They can be any of the following:

▶ **Green**—Means that you are connected to this ActiveList

▶ **Gray**—This ActiveList is offline and you cannot connect to it

▶ **Red**—You are disconnected from the ActiveList, but the ActiveList is online and you can connect if you want

To connect manually to the ActiveList:

1. Right-click the ActiveList you want to connect with.
2. Click Connect.

After a few seconds, you will be connected to the ActiveList. You can start sending and receiving messages to and from the list as soon as you're connected.

Q98 This list is not for me. How can I delete it?

Sometimes, we add an ActiveList out of curiosity, to see exactly what it's all about. But in the end, we realize that the ActiveList is not really for us, and thus we want to get rid of it. Sometimes, an ActiveList can grow so large that the amount of ICQ traffic becomes a bother, at which point you know it's time to stop being a member. To delete an ActiveList:

1. Right-click the **ActiveList name** in your ICQ window.
2. Click **Remove ICQ ActiveList** in the menu.

The ICQ ActiveList will be removed from your Contact List. You will also be removed from the server's list of members. If you want to rejoin the list, you have to request membership to the list once again.

ICQ Tips and Tricks

ICQ is one of those technologies that has so much packed into it that you could spend a good portion of your life learning every nuance, shortcut, and trap. When you learn about a shortcut or find a nasty trap, sharing it with other ICQ users is a good practice. The ICQ Web site has wonderful volunteer communities of ICQ users that help other ICQ users. Now that you've read this book, we dub you an official ICQ power user.

After reading this book, I've become an ICQ power user. What else can I do?

Integrate ICQ into your Web site in new and exciting ways. Not only can you use the IrCQ Java-based chat modules on your Web page or the ICQ communicator that allows users to know whether you are online and to communicate with you, you also can have people use the traditional mailto: URL to send you an ICQ message, without the visitor to your Web page even knowing it.

Remember that one of your ICQ features is the ability to receive ICQ pager messages by e-mail. When you are writing a Web page, you can include a *mailto: tag.* Embedding this tag into a Web page allows visitors to click a link and launch an e-mail client with your e-mail address already filled in.

When you create a mailto: tag for your Web page, instead of adding the same old tired e-mail address, try using **mailto:<*your ICQ number*>@wp.icq.com**. When visitors to your site click this link and fill out the mail message, it will be sent to you as an instant ICQ pager message.

Advanced Web page developers can use some of the form processing utilities to have the results of a form sent to them via e-mail. Of course, anything that can be sent to you by e-mail (except attachments) can be sent to you as an ICQ pager message. We use the Microsoft CDONTS object to send e-mail within our Web scripts. The results of the forms are sent directly to us using ICQ. Our Web visitors are shocked at how quickly we respond to them.

TIP

When you ask for information in a form, don't forget to ask for ICQ numbers, too.

If you are running ICQ within your company to allow your employees to communicate with one another, you might consider installing the ICQ Groupware server. This is a special ICQ server that allows companies to have their employees communicate with one another, no matter where in the world they are located. This ICQ server keeps the ICQ communications private and does not allow communication with the normal Internet-ICQ. It is for internal use only.

CAUTION

ICQ warns that the Groupware server was designed to be small and light and, thus, has sacrificed security features. If security is a concern, you should carefully consider whether you want to use this product. ICQ also recommends not using it for mission-critical applications.

The ICQ Groupware server is primarily for use by small- to medium-sized companies. The license agreement limits you to two hundred users. It also restricts you from providing services to the general public by using this server.

For more information, or to download the ICQ Groupware server, go to **www.icq.com/groupware/**.

Instant messaging is growing, and ICQ, the small company that started it all, has kept the pace, creating new and exciting features and abilities. New instant messengers are popping up every day. One you should watch out for, Jabber, will interoperate with ICQ and is based on the open software standard. Check out **www.jabber.org** for more information about this new development.

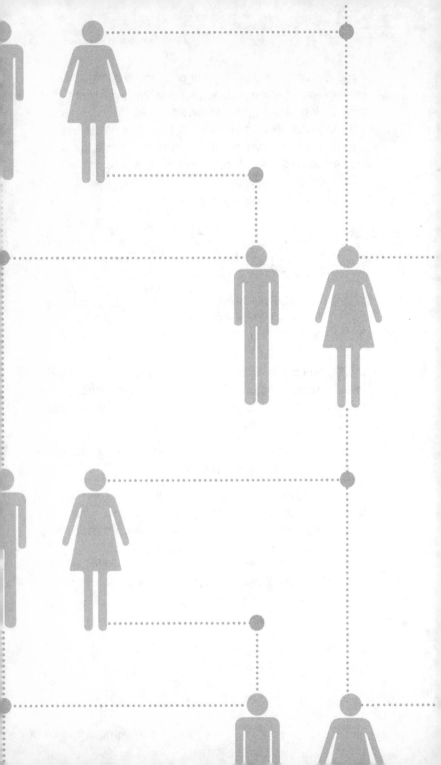

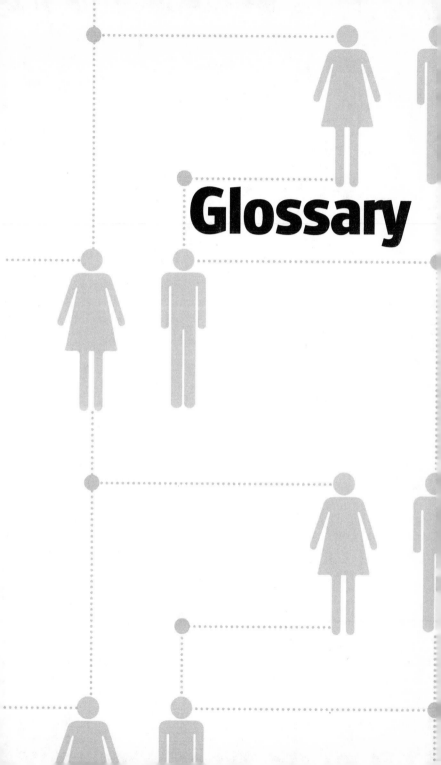

Glossary

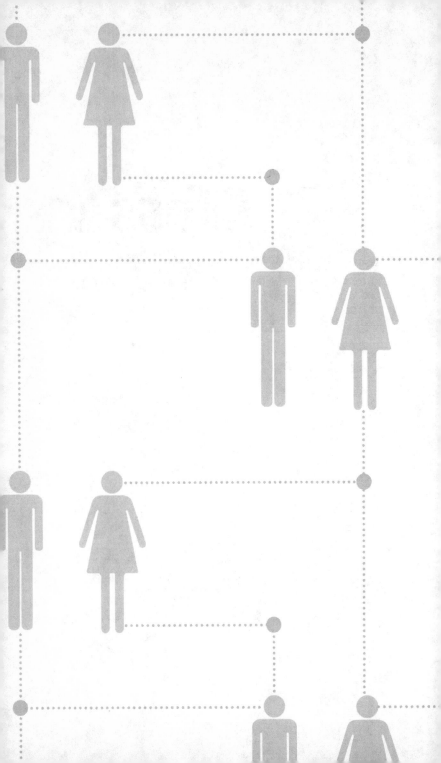

Glossary

ActiveList

An ICQ feature that allows people to belong to a community of ICQ users who share a common interest; allows members of the list to share messages, see their online status, chat as a group or privately, post messages to a message board, and broadcast messages to the group. **See Question 8.**

Archive

A backup copy; to create a backup copy. **See Question 25.**

Background Color

The color that appears behind text. When black text appears on a white page, white is considered the background color. **See Question 29.**

Bigfoot

An Internet company that provides permanent e-mail addresses and an LDAP search engine for locating people. A custom version of ICQ was built for Bigfoot e-mail, Web site, and search engine users. **See Question 16.**

Chat Room

A virtual place, not a physical place, where many people can come together electronically to chat at the same time. **See Question 27.**

CHATMASTER

A person who runs his or her own chat room.
See Question 89.

CONTACT

Person on the Internet with whom you want to communicate.
You can keep a list of these people in your Contact List.

CONTACT LIST

A list within ICQ of the people with whom you regularly
communicate and who have given their permission to view
their online presence. **See Question 10.**

CURSOR

Blinking character that identifies where text will appear next
when typed.

CU-SEEME

A communications program that allows people to send and
receive video over the Internet. CU-SeeMe also has chat
features. **See Question 80.**

DATABASE

Software that stores information, enabling it to be retrieved later.

DEFAULT

A value set initially in a program. Some programs enable you
to reset values to their "factory setting" or default values.

Dialog Box

An informational window, usually smaller than the full screen, that displays or gathers information and then goes away. For example, the Preferences dialog box enables an ICQ user to set or view custom ICQ settings.

Digital Subscriber Line (DSL)

High-speed data line provided by the telephone company for Internet access. **See Question 5.**

Dynamic IP Address

An IP address that is issued by the ISP when you connect to the Internet. Your computer is configured to automatically use the dynamic IP address when it receives it from the ISP.

Dynamic Link Library (DLL)

Files (with a .dll file extension) that contain program functionality required by ICQ, the operating system, and other programs. The program functionality in DLLs can be shared by many programs. **See Question 35.**

Emote

Electronically display an emotion. ICQ has the ability to display emotions electronically while chatting. **See Question 32.**

Enhanced E-mail Check (EEC)

A basic e-mail client for checking and responding to basic e-mail.

Events

Messages, requests or file transfers sent or received within ICQ.

Glossary

FIREWALL

Computer hardware that acts as a gateway between the Internet and a computer or a network of computers. Firewall hardware and software protect computers from unauthorized access by acting as the go-between for all communications to and from the Internet. **See Question 6.**

FOLLOW ME

ICQ feature that allows others to always know the phone number where you can be reached. **See Question 75.**

FONT

The particular style of lettering in which text is displayed. Fonts have names such as Courier, Times New Roman, and Arial.

FONT SIZE

The physical size of the text as it is displayed. **See Question 29.**

FOREGROUND COLOR

The color in which text is displayed. **See Question 30.**

HACKER

Person who attempts to gain unauthorized access to another's computer system or software program. Hacking, considered fun by some, is generally illegal

HOMEPAGE

A MIME document, published using the Web, that usually either stands alone or acts as the top document in a list of documents. Homepages can contain any type of information. **See Question 62.**

HYPERTEXT MARKUP LANGUAGE (HTML)

Programming language in which HTML tags, embedded into the text, instruct Web browsers how to display formatted text. **See Question 62.**

ICON

Small image that represents an operation to perform; for example, the flower icon that appears on the button in the upper-left corner of the ICQ window that changes between Online and Offline mode.

ICQ ("I SEEK YOU")

An Internet communications program that includes instant messaging, chat, e-mail, and integration with other communications programs. **See Question 1.**

ICQ ADDRESS

The long string of numbers that uniquely identifies a particular ICQ user. An ICQ user can have more than one ICQ address. **See Question 5.**

INSTANT MESSENGER

A program, such as ICQ, that allows a person to send and receive messages with others instantly, and usually allows users of the software to know whether others are online or offline. **See Question 2.**

INTERNET RELAY CHAT (IRC)

The original Internet chat program. It is powerful and still in wide use today. ICQ allows you to chat in IRC mode. **See Question 27.**

IP ADDRESS

Unique number that identifies every computer attached to a network such as the Internet. A network uses an IP address to route information to and from computers attached to the network. **See Question 64.**

JAVA

Programming language that can run on any platform where the Java environment (called a Java Virtual Machine) is installed. A version of ICQ is written in Java.

KEYWORD

A word used in a search phrase that will be found in the title or contents of the documents being searched. Searching based on keywords directs a search engine to find documents that include the keyword.

LINK

Short for hyperlink, which can be either text or an image that, when clicked with a mouse, loads a resource over the Internet. Documents containing links to other documents are said to be linked. Linked documents form the basis of the Web.

MAXIMIZE

Cause a window to appear full-screen.

MINIMIZE

Cause a window to disappear from the screen without closing the program. Minimized windows normally leave a reference to themselves at the bottom of the screen, in the taskbar. Clicking the reference causes the window to reappear.

MOUSE POINTER

Not a small hunting dog. The small icon that moves onscreen when you move your mouse. The small icon can change depending on circumstances. For example, during a period when the computer is busy, the mouse pointer may change to an hourglass. When resizing a window, the mouse pointer changes to a double arrow.

Multipurpose Internet Mail Extension (MIME)

Originally a design for extending text mail, it has been adopted by the Web to include more than text. MIME is what made the Web graphically possible.

Musical Instrument Digital Interface (MIDI)

Electronic language "spoken" by musical instruments and synthesizers. A way for musical equipment to communicate.

NetMeeting

Microsoft communications program that enables you to chat, video conference, or communicate using voice features. It also includes the ability to share applications and work together using a whiteboard. **See Question 80.**

Network

Two or more computers connected in a way that enables them to communicate. The Internet is a worldwide network, where each computer connected to the Internet is connected to every other computer connected to the Internet.

Network Lag

Also known as the "World Wide Wait" when referring to the Internet, this is the time it takes for information to travel across the network.

Plug-ins

Programs that add features and extend the functionality of larger programs; can be installed into ICQ and other programs that can have their functionality extended in this manner. **See Question 35.**

Post Office Protocol version 3 (POP3)

The protocol that e-mail programs use to check your e-mail. See also Simple Mail Transport Protocol.

Glossary

Power PC

A computer created from an IBM-Motorola-Apple alliance, the hope of which was to create a universal operating system for the home.

Preferences

User-configurable choices that customize the way a program looks or operates.

Proxy Server

A computer program through which all of your Internet communications travel. Some proxy servers are designed to direct Internet traffic to and from computers on a network that is not configured to communicate with the Internet directly. A proxy server can also be configured as a firewall. **See Question 6.**

Recipient

Person on the ICQ network to whom you are sending a message.

Search Engine

A program, usually running on a Web page, that allows people to search a database of indexed pages, newsgroups, or people directories. The search engine returns a list of document titles and URLs, and a brief description of each item.

Server

A computer that runs software that provides a service, such as a Web server or an ICQ server. Server programs listen for incoming requests from client programs, such as the ICQ program or a Web browser, and then process the clients' requests.

SHORTCUT

A special key or combination of keys that performs a task that would normally take many keystrokes. Or, an icon on your desktop that you can click to launch the corresponding program, instead of selecting the program from the Start menu.

SHUT DOWN

Instructing Microsoft Windows, the Mac OS, or the UNIX OS to close all programs and either shut off or restart the computer. You should always select the Shut Down option when turning off a computer.

SIMPLE MAIL TRANSPORT PROTOCOL (SMTP)

The protocol that allows your e-mail program to send e-mail. See also Post Office Protocol version 3.

SKINS

Special graphical overlays that enable you to customize the look and feel of computer programs, some of which can take on an entirely different appearance. Add-on programs are available that enable you to change the appearance of ICQ by using skins. **See Question 56.**

SOUND CARD

A computer expansion card that comes standard in almost all computers that play complex sounds, such as sounds from music CDs, MP3 files, and WAV files. In many cases, sound cards have the ability to create their own sounds by using the Musical Instrument Digital Interface (MIDI) commands. **See Question 36.**

Glossary

Spam

A canned meat product of the Hormel Corporation. Spam also refers to unsolicited messages and e-mail, usually part of an anonymous mass-marketing effort. Spamming on ICQ is considered extremely discourteous and is highly discouraged. **See Question 38.**

Tab

A graphical device that appears on a dialog box similar to how the small tab extension of a manila file folder appears in a filing cabinet; you can view each tab's information simply by clicking the tab, without switching windows.

Tag

Character(s) between angle brackets (< and >), inserted into a Web page to instruct the Web browser how particular text in that page should be displayed. Tags are also known as markup tags. **See Question 62.**

Telephony

Adjective used to describe a wide array of communications technologies; originally referred strictly to telephone technologies. Its exact meaning is less clear today.

Uniform (or Universal) Resource Locator (URL)

The address of a resource located on a network such as the Internet. All URLs are unique and identify documents and services.

User

A person using a computer or network resource. Users in ICQ are also known as contacts.

WEB SITE

A document or related documents, usually written in HTML, available through the Web. The documents that make up a Web site are also known as Web pages.

WHITE PAGES

A directory of Internet contact information similar to the telephone white pages from which these directories derive their name. **See Question 15.**

WINDOW

A framed, rectangular area of the screen in a windowed OS, such as Microsoft Windows, UNIX and Linux X Window System, and the Macintosh OS. A program running in a windowed environment runs in its own window or windows. The window normally has a title bar and optional menus that allow you to close, minimize, and maximize the window. Windows can also have horizontal and vertical scroll bars for viewing parts of the program that extend beyond the window frame.

WORLD WIDE WEB

A system of Internet servers that support specially formatted documents, which can be retrieved by using Web browsers. These documents can contain links to other documents. The idea of the Web grew from an earlier project involving hyperlinked documents.

Glossary

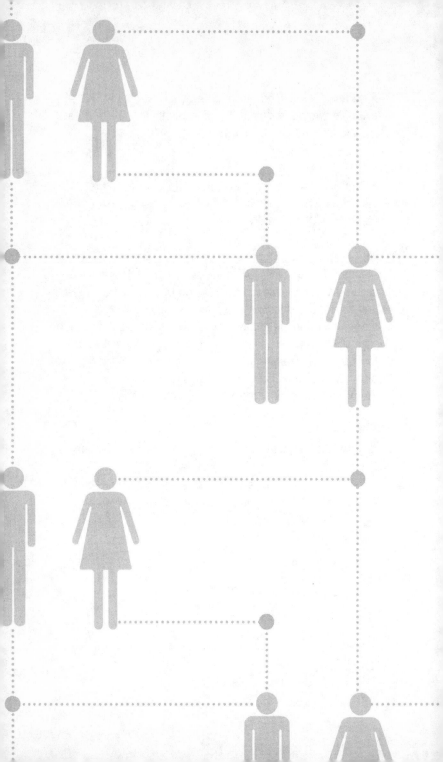

Index

R

S

W

X

Y

Z

Order our free catalog by visiting
http://www.muskalipman.com

Order Form

Postal Orders:
Muska & Lipman Publishing
P.O. Box 8225
Cincinnati, Ohio 45208

On-Line Orders or more information:
http://www.muskalipman.com
Fax Orders:
(513) 924-9333

Qty.	Title	ISBN	Price	Total Cost
_____	*MP3 FYI*	1-929685-05-X	$14.95	_____
_____	*iMac FYI*	1-929685-06-8	$14.95	_____
_____	*Genealogy Basics Online*	1-929685-00-9	$24.95	_____
_____	*Digital Camera Solutions*	0-9662889-6-3	$29.95	_____
_____	*Scanner Solutions*	0-9662889-7-1	$29.95	_____

Subtotal _____

Sales Tax _____
(please add 6% for books shipped to Ohio addresses)

Shipping _____
($5.00 for US and Canada, $10.00 other countries)

TOTAL PAYMENT ENCLOSED _____

Ship to:

Company _____

Name _____

Address _____

City _____

State _____ Zip _____ Country _____

E-mail _____

Educational facilities, companies, and organizations interested in multiple copies of these books should contact the publisher for quantity discount information. Training manuals, CD-ROMs, electronic versions, and portions of these books are also available individually or can be tailored for specific needs.

Thank you for your order.